LIVING LITURGY

ELEMENTARY REFLECTIONS

TRANSLATED FROM THE ITALIAN
BY PATRICIA A. COULTER AND
JULIE COULTER-ENGLISH

Catechesis of
the Good Shepherd
Publications

Acknowledgments

All scripture quotations are taken from the *New Revised Standard Version* of the Bible © 1989 Division of Christian Education of the National Council of the Churches of Christ of the United States of America. All rights reserved.

Excerpts from the *Rite of Consecrating the Chrism* © 1972 International Committee on English in the Liturgy, Inc. All rights reserved.

Text © 1998 Catechesis of the Good Shepherd.

LIVING LITURGY: ELEMENTARY REFLECTIONS © 1998 Archdiocese of Chicago: Liturgy Training Publications, 1800 North Hermitage Avenue, Chicago IL 60622-1101; 1-800-933-1800; fax 1-800-933-7094; orders@ltp.org; www.ltp.org. All rights reserved.

This book was edited by Heinz R. Kuehn, with assistance from Victoria M. Tufano. Deborah Bogaert was the production editor. The book was designed by Lisa Buckley, and Karen Mitchell was the production artist. The typeface used is Minion. Printed by Webcom Limited of Toronto, Canada.

Library of Congress Catalog Card Number: 98-65273

06 05 04 03 02   6 5 4 3 2

Catechesis of the Good Shepherd Publications is an imprint of Liturgy Training Publications (LTP). Further information about these publications is available from LTP or from the Catechesis of the Good Shepherd, PO Box 1084, Oak Park IL 60304; 708-524-1210; fax 708-386-8032. Requests for information about other aspects of the Catechesis should be directed to this address.

OTHER CATECHESIS OF THE GOOD SHEPHERD BOOKS

The Catechesis of the Good Shepherd in a Parish Setting
Tina L. Lillig

Discovering the Real Spiritual Life of Children (video)
Sofia Cavalletti and Silvana Q. Montanaro

The Good Shepherd and the Child: A Joyful Journey
Sofia Cavalletti, Patricia Coulter, Gianna Gobbi and
Silvana Q. Montanaro (also available in Spanish)

History's Golden Thread: The History of Salvation
Sofia Cavalletti

Journals of the Catechesis of the Good Shepherd 1984–1997

The Religious Potential of the Child
Sofia Cavalletti (also available in Spanish)

Contents

Foreword

LITURGY IS THE SUMMIT AND SOURCE OF THE LIFE of the church. We Christians are supposed to live it every day, from birth to death. Often we do not realize sufficiently how much treasure is hidden behind the words and symbols that make up the liturgical events. Since the events are composed of the word of God and are expressed by symbols, the full extent of the liturgy will reach us only if from early childhood we are exposed to the wonderful panorama of these symbols and the language of the liturgy. The much expected liturgical renewal depends upon how much we are able to assimilate these into our spiritual life.

For this reason I welcome the English translation of Sofia Cavalletti's *Living Liturgy*. Ms. Cavalletti is well qualified to bring close to us the theological and liturgical depth of the rites, words and symbols. Her liturgico-theological expertise and her pedagogical experience with the Montessori method provide the guarantee that we have here something important, presented to us in simple, understandable language, for catechists and, ultimately, for children.

Therefore I recommend this book with great pleasure to all who want to drink fresh water from the fountain of the Christian liturgy.

Attila Mikloshazy, SJ, STD
Ep. tit. Castellominoritanus
Professor of Systematic Theology and Liturgy
Dean, St. Augustine's Seminary
Toronto School of Theology

Introduction

THE FOLLOWING PAGES ARE THE RESULT OF MANY
years of experience teaching adults as well as children, whom
I began to instruct when they were still at a very young age.
To many it will seem unusual that it was above all the experience
with children — and with the youngest children — that has
helped me to draft these pages without losing any of the theological wealth of the themes presented here.

Let me explain. In this book I wish to present certain
elementary themes basic to the study of liturgy in the hope
that they might assist in increasing an awareness of and active
participation in the celebration of the liturgy and might eventually serve as a springboard for further study. In using the term
elementary I do not mean lacking substance. On the contrary,
by *elementary* I would like to indicate a core of essential themes,
elements that reside at the deepest level, which act as a departure
point so as to reach ever-expanding horizons. I want to affirm
the conviction that simplicity is found in the elementary and
that the greatest of realities are simple and essential. Simplicity
and essentiality are inseparable and are characteristic of what
is most profound. Is there anything simpler, more essential, than
a morsel of bread, a few drops of wine? And yet, it is by means
of these that the Christian community lives its greatest realities.
It is through simplicity that we attain profundity.

If we were to focus on the fundamental elements of the
liturgy and to contemplate them in themselves without allowing
ourselves to be distracted by peripheral matters, then they
would disclose to us unfathomable depths capable of nourishing
our Christian life with the most nutritious food. These basic
elements contain within themselves something like a highly

concentrated light, capable of illuminating the Christian mystery in its depth and breadth. Sometimes, though, the genuine concern for knowledge can degenerate into intellectualism and obscure this light. I have tried to steer clear of this danger in these pages.

This statement may sound very ambitious. Only the eagle can look directly into the sun, and here, within these few pages, I am claiming to focus on the essential aspects of the Christian mystery as they are lived in the liturgy.

I would like to justify this claim with the authority of an expert: the young child. I mentioned that in drafting this work I have been guided primarily by the young child. I have approached the Christian mystery together with young children in the conviction that when we have not succeeded in handing on what is essential to the littlest — be they "little" because of chronological age or cultural preparation — it means that it is we who have not managed to reach the nucleus, that we have lingered upon elements of secondary importance, the kind that do not really nurture life.

It is the young child who has been my true teacher in reaching this nucleus, because the younger the children, the more essential their vital needs. My experience has taught me that some aspects leave little children untouched, whereas others are taken hold of by children from a variety of environments and cultures. Certain elements call forth a response of theological depth and serious joy in children and are received with delight, thereby becoming the inalienable inheritance of their spiritual lives. This is how young children have come to be my guides, exacting and rigorous guides who constantly challenge me, in Dante's words, to "Let your words be counted," and who withdraw their attention the instant I distance myself from what is essential.

I have come to realize that the themes to which children respond in the way I have just described — though the children come from very different environments and cultures — constitute the very nucleus of the Christian message.

In this way, a *curriculum* started to take shape, one defined by some of the ABCs of Christianity, which are of the same fundamental and indispensable value that ABCs are in every form of communication.

It is a *curriculum* formed by uninterrupted study and research, one that has shown itself to be valid in relation to both adults and children. In fact, I recognized that what the children had pointed out to me are actually the elements that have remained the most enduring and vibrant in the life of the church from its earliest beginnings. Thus I have seen with joy how young children, Christianity's newest recruits, spontaneously insert themselves into the rich river of tradition while directing me to it as the source from which to draw sustenance for our lives.

With this essential nucleus as my starting point — the ABCs I mentioned — individual themes were then singled out and developed with older children and with adults. However, with the youngest child, the deepest core had already been touched upon, which afterward opened into the broader exploration of more specialized studies.

Nevertheless, working with the young child requires extremely demanding preparation in order to remain rooted in that level of essentiality that corresponds to the young child's own nature. It is not a case of trivializing matters: With the young child it is necessary to prune away those secondary elements and details that may represent easy evasions.

One further word about the language I use with young children: Since I obviously could not adopt the vocabulary of textbooks and treatises, it was not difficult for me to realize that I had another language at my disposal, the one liturgy has always spoken — the language of signs. I will not develop this point here, both because it is a generally known fact and because it will be addressed in what follows. The language of liturgy — signs or symbols — is one that speaks to the learned and to the unlearned, to adults and to children. It is a language that one both hears and *sees;* it invites us into an immediate and living contact with the reality presented. It is an allusive language that does not pretend to enclose the Christian mystery within the limits of an enunciation and respects the level of growth of each individual believer. It is a language that attracts us, I could even say seduces us (Jeremiah 20:7), drawing us to ponder — with eyes, heart and mind — what it is expressing and to marvel in seeing how its content opens onto ever deepening and widening horizons.

I have been able to see how children grasp the meaning of this language with ease, with depth, with joy. I have seen how they use it spontaneously in making comparisons among various themes and in connecting them. I have seen how adults are captivated by this language no less than children when faced with its inexhaustibly evocative force.

It is my hope that in the following pages I have been able to stay on that level of essentiality which the children have taught me.

Sofia Cavalletti
Rome, Easter, 1995

PART ONE

Foundations

ALL BELONGS TO YOU,

AND YOU BELONG TO CHRIST,

AND CHRIST BELONGS TO GOD.

1 CORINTHIANS 3:22 – 23

Liturgy in the Cosmic Plan of God

THERE HAS ALWAYS BEEN A PLAN IN GOD'S MIND, one leading all persons and all creation to fullness. The first book of the Bible, with its two accounts of creation, speaks to us of the original realization of that plan. The last book of the Bible, the book of Revelation, shows us future realities, the "mystery of the will" of God (Ephesians 1:9ff), which will be fulfilled when God will be all in all (1 Corinthians 15:28). The time from creation to parousia — the time in which we live — is the time of history that flows into the full realization of the kingdom of God. From creation to parousia is the time when the kingdom is being built through God's initiative, which seeks out humankind because it is with humanity that God's plan will be accomplished.

The range of God's plan is cosmic, embracing all things that are in heaven and on earth (Ephesians 1:10). And "every creature in heaven and on earth and under the earth and in the sea, and all that is in them" is called to participate in the universal praise of God (Revelation 5:13). In this all-encompassing framework of time and space, what is liturgy's function during the period of history in which we are living?

In order to understand this point, it might be helpful to pause a moment and ponder the work of the creation of the world. Let's imagine that we were witnesses to this: We saw the formless world being born, and then we saw it gradually take shape and become organized. We saw vegetable and animal life begin. With admiration we contemplated the world as it grew continually more beautiful, and, moved by wonder, we asked ourselves, "Why? What is the purpose of all this?"

Despite everything, the world would have given us the impression of being static and incomplete. For example, what is the use of a fossil forest if no one can profit from it? Who will mine the coal hidden in the depths of the earth if no one is capable of getting it out? Who is able to enjoy the beauty of flowers? How could a fibrous plant such as cotton or flax reach the purpose inherent in its nature? At the beginning of the sixth day of creation, the world is finished and incomplete at one and the same time. A certain perfection has been achieved, but it is still waiting for something. It is waiting for someone.

When creation was completed, "God created human-kind in his image, in the image of God he created them; male and female he created them" (Genesis 1:27). Having made the world full of wonderful things, God now places it in the hands of human creatures so that they will fill it with their industrious presence, so that they will "have dominion over the fish of the sea and over the birds of the air and over every living thing that moves upon the earth" (Genesis 1:28). Creation is entrusted to the human creatures so that they will "till it and keep it" (Genesis 2:15). Creation was waiting for human creatures so that its components could achieve the purpose for which they were created, so that everything would become dynamic and have meaning.

Creation was waiting for human creatures, for their capacity to enjoy and work in the world in order to transform it and slowly bring it to completion. Human creatures, by their own work, take possession of the earth's goods, have dominion over them — according to the words of Genesis — while at the same time making it possible for these goods to carry out the tasks assigned to them in God's great plan. This phenome-non continues today before our eyes as we see elements of nature we considered devoid of usefulness which, refined by human effort, render great service to humanity. For example, penicillin is a mold, strictly a waste component of nature. Once it came into contact with the human spirit, we can say that it changed its state and acquired meaning; it achieved its goal.

With the human creature on the scene, we are now able to answer the question we asked ourselves: Why creation? It was given to the created or subhuman world[1] to reach a level that in some way transcends it; with the appearance of man and woman, it is fulfilled. By means of their diligent hands, the various elements of the world find their fulfillment and assume a place and significance in the universe of creation, which somehow raises the created world above the level it occupied before the appearance of man and woman.

Now our question shifts and is expressed like this: Why man and woman? Would human creatures be restricted to their own level — however high and exalted — and thus be shut off from the possibility of access to a level of greater fulfillment and richer meaning? If so, these creatures that crown creation would be in a position inferior to irrational creatures. They would be denied the possibility that subhuman creatures have. Is there not a passage open to human beings leading to a higher world? Will they not be given wings to fly above their own human world?

THE MEDIATOR OF OUR WORK

Obviously the answer is yes, and we know that the world that opens up to humanity is the world of God. Human beings, however, are not able to penetrate it by their own powers alone. The subhuman world needs someone to bring it to fulfillment. This someone has to be the human creature, who, while physiologically belonging to the lower world and at the same time transcending it as a rational being, thus establishes a kind of bridge between the subhuman world and the world of humanity.

Humanity too needs a mediator in order to enter the world of God. That is, humanity needs a person who belongs both to the world of God and to our own human world and therefore is in a position to join these two shores together. This person is the God-Man, Jesus, whose function is eminently that of mediator. It will be a special kind of work that will effect humanity's attainment of its true purpose and also its becoming part of God's world. This particular kind of work is called *worship* or *liturgy,* a term that means precisely *work.* It is significant that Hebrew, Greek and Latin, all languages which form the basis of our civilization, use the same word for work and worship. This demonstrates a substantial affinity between these two activities even though they are performed on different planes. Worship is the work that we human creatures do but cannot carry out by ourselves; we can do it only when the "sap" of God runs in our veins (John 15). It is work we perform when new wings are given to us as a gift for the conquest, not only of this world but of the divine world as well. It is work we can perform when we are given new capabilities, new potential, and these capabilities and potential are God's life in us.

Just as in the garden of Eden, where man and woman were called to work, so too throughout human history we have been called to worship God, becoming whole and complete not only on the natural, human plane, but on the supernatural or divine level as well.

In the worship of God, we bring our whole lives with us, even that activity in which we use and enjoy the goods of this world. In worship we also bring elements of the lower scale of nature with us that are transformed by the work of our hands and mind. In worship, the human person brings what Paul synthesizes by calling it "all." Therefore, in worship the vital circuit is completed: "All belong to you, and you belong to Christ, and Christ belongs to God" (1 Corinthians 3:22 – 23). The person who carries within "all" the goods of this world becomes part of Jesus, and Jesus "is God's." Thus, worship which the human creature performs in Christ makes us part of him, consecrates us to God. And in worship, the human creature, through Christ, consecrates the whole universe to God. The action that worship enacts is cosmic. It is not restricted to the human world but reaches all that is created in its depth and breadth, reinstating the harmony that reigned in creation before humanity disrupted it with sin.

Liturgy in the Biblical Tradition: The Memorial

THE PEOPLE OF GOD — THE HEBREW AND CHRISTIAN branches — has its own way of living liturgy because it has its own way of living history. In the biblical tradition, history is the place of the encounter with God. God is present in all history, but throughout the course of this history, certain events have assumed special importance as particular manifestations of God's eternal will to bring the human creature to the fullness of completion. There are events in the biblical tradition that have taken on the nature of a paradigm of God's will for salvation.

Let us consider the main events: creation, the choosing of the Jewish people in the person of Abraham, the liberation of the chosen people in the Exodus, the incarnation of the Son of God in the midst of this people, and the death and resurrection of Christ. In Christ, God's plan reaches a fullness which is not, however, intended to be confined only to his person; rather, it will embrace all humanity and the whole of creation.

The major points in the history of salvation are therefore creation, the calling of the patriarchs, the Exodus, the incarnation and the parousia. All these events took place in the past, with the exception of the parousia; the parousia is still something we are hoping for and awaiting. A historical occurrence is bound by the time and place in which it happened; if I was not there, I am still able to know about it and recall it, but I cannot truly participate in it. Not even the death and resurrection of Jesus can escape this law: Christ's death and resurrection is a historical event that occurred on a certain day, in a certain place, outside the walls of Jerusalem. And I was not there.

Does that mean that I am irremediably cut off, forever left out of the event that is the foundational event of our salvation? Faced with this particular presence of God in the midst of humanity, should I say: It was a marvelous thing, but I was born too late? Could I, living now, somehow manage to get into that flow of divine life that the death and resurrection of Christ brought into the world? Jewish believers could address a similar question to themselves: How is it possible now, after about two and a half thousand years, to be participants in the liberation that the God of Abraham, of Isaac and of Jacob worked for the people of Israel? How can Jews living today be freed in the same way Moses and his contemporaries were?

THE TODAY OF LITURGY

The Jew finds the answer in the Passover ritual (the *haggadah* of Passover, to which we will return later), where it is written: "Every Jew must consider oneself as having come out of Egypt," that is, as actually present at the moment of liberation.

The Christian who in the eucharist proclaims the "mystery of faith" does not only articulate two past events — the death and resurrection — and the coming of Christ in glory, which lies in the future. The Christian's "mystery of faith" is the presence, the *today* of the supreme event of the life of Jesus, the Christ, which offers each one of us who comes into history the possibility of taking part in it.

Thus, rewording in Christian terms the Jewish liturgical passage just cited, we could say: "Let every Christian consider oneself as actually present at the death and resurrection of Christ." In proclaiming the mystery of faith, the Christian points to that which one is doing in this present celebration as well as to that which one expects to occur in the future.

Liturgy as an act of the human creature and also, most importantly, as an act of God, frees the historical occurrence from its limits in time and space and constantly re-presents it throughout all time. In this way, persons of every age, as each one enters into history, can become active participants in this event and can enjoy the richness of divine life that springs forth from it. We can say that liturgy takes the historical event it is celebrating and pulls it out of the time and place where it happened in order to make it present, offering to every person the possibility of becoming actively involved in it.

This is the way the people of the biblical tradition live history in the liturgy. Liturgy is the *memorial* of the events of salvation. *Memorial* does not mean memory, the mental process by which I go back to some past happening and think about it today in a subjective way. *Memorial* renders the event it celebrates objectively present, thereby making it possible for me to participate in it today. The memorial is an objective reality, a fact that is being actualized objectively, today.

Exodus 12, with its prescriptions for the celebration of the Pasch, recalls the events of the coming out of Egypt and says: "*This* day [of celebration] shall be a day of remembrance for you. You shall celebrate it as a festival to the LORD throughout your generations" (v. 14). As the proclamation is given to new generations, each Jew must say that the celebration takes place "because of what the LORD did for me when I came out of Egypt" (Exodus 13:8). Deuteronomy 5:3 is even more explicit: "Not with our ancestors did the LORD make this covenant, but with us, who are all of us here alive today."

The Christian eucharistic liturgy also expresses the meaning of the celebration in an explicit way with the words: "Father, we now celebrate this memorial of our redemption. We recall Christ's death . . . his resurrection . . . and, looking forward to his coming in glory, we offer. . . ."[2] Because we are present and actively participating today in the death and resurrection of Christ, we can do with him today what he has done and still does: We are able to *offer*. The memorial is the *actualization* of the historical events that without it would be solely in the past and hence unreachable for us. In the celebration, these events become *actual*. The memorial, therefore, shows itself to be free from the restrictions of time and space. In the liturgical celebration, the human person lives that freedom.

We ask ourselves now if this freedom pertains only to the past, that is, whether liturgy breaks through the limits of time and space only with respect to the past, or if we can say that this is true in relation to the future as well. What place does eschatology occupy in the liturgical celebration? Is it only something to be longed for with desire and hope, and as such only an inner subjective attitude? Or is the fullness we are waiting to be completed at the end of time in some way being realized already, here and now, in the liturgical celebration? Is liturgy only an actualization of the past, or is it also an anticipation of the future? Is the future an insurmountable barrier for the liturgy?

We will try to find answers by once again considering the paradigmatic points of biblical history we mentioned above and seeing how they are lived in the Jewish and Christian traditions.

We will begin with creation. The memorial of creation has a particular place in the Jewish liturgy for the Sabbath. We read in the prayer for the Sabbath evening: "Thus the heavens and the earth were finished . . ." (Genesis 2:1); and at the conclusion of this domestic ritual in the home,[3] there is a prayer that blesses the Lord for giving the Sabbath — "the memorial of the work of creation" — as an inheritance to the people of Israel. Abstaining from work — a very important element of the festive day — is connected with the creation, which God gave humanity as a gift, a totally gratuitous gift.[4] The Sabbath is the *sign* of the fact that the Lord made the heavens and the earth for the human creature, and the one who keeps the Sabbath is giving witness to it. On the day of Sabbath, we are to enjoy creation free from all duty except that of praising God. Consequently, the Sabbath liturgy is full of praise and thanksgiving for what we are now enjoying in creation.

However, the Sabbath liturgy does not stop merely with invoking the past that is being enjoyed in the present. In the thanksgiving for food, especially, one turns toward the future in the many invocations of the coming of the Messiah and of that day which the Merciful One will give to Israel, that day which will be "all Sabbath and rest in life everlasting."[5] The Jew, then, who celebrates the Sabbath is linked through the present fruition of goods gratuitously given to the beginning of creation and is living already, though temporarily for now, the eschatological day in which all that makes the Sabbath a special day will have no more limits.

> The Sabbath is a reminder of two worlds: this world and the future one — it is an example of both worlds. The Sabbath is actually joy, holiness and rest; joy is part of this world, holiness and rest are part of the future world![6]

The past, present and future, therefore, all have a basis in the celebration.

Another cardinal point in biblical history is the calling of the patriarchs and the covenant which the Lord made with Abraham. The patriarchs are frequently mentioned in Jewish liturgy because through them, Israel today becomes, in a special way, part of that relationship with God that began with Abraham. During the celebration of circumcision, there is a prayer of blessing to the Lord "who commanded us to bring [the child] into the covenant of Abraham our father." Circumcision is the moment when the Jew is joined to what happened between Abraham and God about 1800 years before Christ, enabling the child who is born today to live that covenant and thus making that covenant forever actual. Here too there is no stopping at just the present and the past. One only needs to look at the importance given in this celebration to the "throne of Elijah," the prophet who is considered the precursor of the Messiah. The hymn that concludes the liturgy (and dates from the eleventh century) prays:

> May God send us his faultless Messiah . . .
> May God send us Elijah the true priest,
> Concealed till his bright throne be ready . . .[7]

Here, too, the liturgy is taken as *memorial,* the actualization of a past event reaching out toward the end of history.

Moving on to the Exodus, another cardinal moment in the history of Israel, we have already quoted a passage from the Passover liturgy that highlights the importance for every Jew to remain present, now, to that faraway moment. As we will see more clearly further on, all the ritual elements (unleavened bread, bitter herbs, lamb) of the Passover celebration tend to re-create the conditions of the Exodus so that the Jew today can participate in it. The eschatological tension is very prominent in this celebration, and it is expressed by the repeated invocation that the Messiah "come quickly to our days" (see The Jewish Passover Banquet, page 73).

Thus, liturgy is always articulated in the three dimensions of past, present and future because this is biblical time, time which is not a fragment but a "chain"[8] held together by the thought of God. "The present event is like a taut rope that cannot be imagined without knots of impact in the past and future"[9] because time is history, and history is the realization of God's plan, and liturgy is the particular way in which people of the biblical tradition live history. In every celebration, all of history, in a concentrated form, is lived, although in every celebration a certain event in particular is highlighted.

In some sense, as we mentioned already, this is common both to Jews and to Christians. In fact, if we look at Christian liturgy we will find there the same movement in time. The prayer for the consecration of the water during the rite of baptism goes back to creation, enumerates the principal events of *past* history, and asks the Father to send the Spirit now, today, to vivify the water in the font, so that "all who have died through the baptism in his death will rise again to life with him." Those present are asked to make an explicit profession of faith in the "resurrection of the body and life everlasting." The candle given to the one being baptized points out that this person is a "child of light," and it is given so as to be able to "go out to meet the Lord who comes with all the saints in the heavenly kingdom."

Eucharistic Prayer IV also begins with creation, mentioning several essential elements of past history. As already mentioned, even the death and resurrection we proclaim would be merely a recollection of past deeds if the celebration did not actualize them as we turn toward eschatological waiting: "looking forward to your coming." The "all glory and honor" that concludes all the eucharistic prayers is the expression of cosmic praise that all creatures give, together with the Mother of God, the apostles and saints, to the Father "through, with and in" Christ for ever and ever. The "Amen" with which we conclude the eucharistic prayer is the inclusion, today, of our own voice in that chorus of praise, a chorus in which we are waiting for the participation of "every creature in heaven and on earth and under the earth and in the sea, and all that is in them" (Revelation 5:13).

From the Jewish viewpoint, the Christian celebrates a new event which, the Christian believes, leads to union with God in the person of Jesus the Christ. Nonetheless, the method by which both the Christian and the Jew live history in the liturgical celebration is the same. Christians and Jews are living in a period of rupture, considering the events that already have been realized in history, even though not yet to their fullest: The redemption of Israel happens in the Exodus; the redemption of Christians is in Jesus Christ. Yet Jews and Christians have a point of meeting in turning together in hope toward that moment when the Christ "will come," according to the Jews, and "will come again," according to Christians. The period of rupture begins to mend as Jews and Christians strain toward that moment: "The longed-for Messiah, then, is not merely a point of divergence, but he who somehow is already reuniting one with the other in that shared waiting."[10]

Liturgy in the Christian Tradition: The Priesthood of Christ

HAVING CONSIDERED THE PLACE AND FUNCTION OF liturgy in the cosmos and in history, and having seen how it is lived in the biblical tradition, we ask ourselves: Who performs the liturgy? Who are the actors in the liturgical celebration?

The whole of Christian tradition proclaims the centrality of the person of Christ in the cosmos and in history. The purpose of Christ's coming into the world is the divinization of humanity, a process in which the entire cosmos is involved because it originates from the human body of Christ. The risen body of Christ "is the firstfruits not only of humanity but of all creation."[11] Heaven and earth are united in the sacred humanity of Christ, in that person who by right belongs to two worlds: the world of God and the world of humanity. Christ possesses, in the uniqueness of his person, the divine and human nature. This mystery is called the hypostatic union.

At the center of the history of salvation, Jesus appears essentially as unifier and mediator. A communion comes about in Christ that we can call *vertical,* that is, between God and humanity, to which is added a communion we can call *horizontal,* that is, among persons in Christ. Furthermore, in Christ all the power lines of past history converge, and all those of the future emanate from him.

This comprehensive function has been seen to be symbolized in the figure of the cross itself, which rises toward heaven, penetrates the depths of the earth and embraces east and west. Thus in Christ we have those "firstfruits" of the cosmic communion that will be the complete accomplishment of God's plan. Jesus speaks of his mediating and unifying function, which can be defined as his priestly function, even though this aspect of Christ is not abundantly evident in the New Testament except in the Letter to the Hebrews, where it becomes central.

That letter was addressed to a group of Jews who had recognized the Messiah, the Son of God, in Jesus of Nazareth, and who, perhaps after an early period of enthusiasm, were going through a time of doubt and discouragement. The text refers to the Temple liturgy as a present reality (10:1 – 3), and as such would have had to precede the destruction of the Temple in AD 70.

As well as establishing the bond between Christ the priest and Moses (3:2) and Aaron (5:4), this letter, given its nature and audience, tends to underline the differences between the Hebraic Levite priesthood and the priesthood of Christ. A unity exists between the Old and New testaments, yet in the priesthood of Christ certain traits are specified that constitute something absolutely new.

While in the Levite priesthood a man becomes a priest by right of birth if he is born into the tribe of Levi, Jesus, who belongs to the tribe of Judah, is a priest by "the power of an indestructible life" (Hebrews 7:16), that is, by being the Son of the Father who is made human. Christ is a priest by right. He, and only he, is in the ideal position to build the bridge which unites God's world with the world of humanity. In order to establish himself as mediator between humanity and the Father, Jesus, who is God, had to become in every way like us, as if for this purpose it was not enough to be God. Jesus came, it says in the Letter to the Hebrews, not to help angels but rather "the descendants of Abraham" (2:16), and so he had to assume all the poverty of human flesh — except sin — in order to become "a merciful and faithful high priest in the service of God, to make a sacrifice of atonement for the sins of the people" (2:17).

The priesthood of Christ is eternal: While "there were many priests" (the priests of the Old Testament), "they were prevented by death from continuing in office," whereas the risen Jesus lives forever and is always interceding for humanity (7:25). Christ "entered once for all into the sanctuary" and "not with the blood of goats and calves, but with his own blood" (9:11ff). The offering he makes to the Father is not something outside his person; rather, it is his very self. As such, the sacrifice of Christ is unique and does not have to be repeated. The multiplicity of victims offered by the Levite priesthood would seem to betray an anxiety about the insufficiency of what was being offered, "but when Christ had offered for all time a single sacrifice for sins, 'he sat down at the right hand of God,' and since then has been waiting 'until his enemies would be made a footstool for his feet'" (10:12 – 14).

---

1. By the term "subhuman world" I mean everything in the created world that belongs to a level inferior to, or lower than, the human level.

2. Eucharistic Prayer IV.

3. *Daily Prayer Book* (New York: Hebrew Publishing Company, 1977), 221ff.

4. See A. J. Heschel, *The Sabbath: Its Meaning for Modern Man* (New York: The Noonday Press, 1989).

5. *Daily Prayer Book,* 768.

6. A. J. Heschel, *The Sabbath,* 19.

7. *Daily Prayer Book,* 750.

8. A. Neher, *L'Existence Juive* (Paris: Seuil, 1962), 18.

9. Ibid., 32.

10. *Toward Christian Unity* (Diocese of Rome, 1983), v. 140.

11. C. Vagaggini, OSB, *The Flesh, Instrument of Salvation* (Staten Island: Alba House, 1969), 140.

PART TWO

Living Liturgy

I AM THE VINE,

YOU ARE THE BRANCHES.

THOSE WHO ABIDE IN ME

AND I IN THEM

BEAR MUCH FRUIT,

BECAUSE APART FROM ME

YOU CAN DO NOTHING.

JOHN 15:5

The People of God

THE RISEN JESUS CHRIST, AS PRIEST, IS THE ESSENTIAL
protagonist of the liturgy. Christ joins the people of God to
himself in the celebration. Now we ask ourselves: Who are the
people we call the people of God? On what basis can they
be defined as such? We know that different people are defined
according to common history, language, culture and customs.
In the Christian vision, what is it that, in the people of God,
corresponds to these cohesive components? To find the answer,
we must speak about the doctrine that since the Middle Ages
we have been accustomed to calling the "Mystical Body." By this
we mean the reality of the union of Christ with his people.

In the Gospel of John (15:1 – 10), Jesus is spoken of as
the "true vine," the Father as the vinegrower and we as branches
of the vine. Jesus does not say that he is part — perhaps the
most important part — of the plant but that he is the vine as a
whole, the vine of which we too are part. It is obvious that
the same sap, the same life force, runs in every branch of the same
plant. In Jesus and in us, then, there is the same life, which is
the life of God given to us as a gift, which we call "grace." Its
presence in us is essential in order to be alive in communion
with God; it is just as necessary as sap is for the life of plants and
blood is for bodily life.

The necessity for the Christian to remain united with
Christ is stressed by the frequent repetition of the word
"remain" or "abide" (Greek: *meno*), which occurs ten times in
ten verses. For the best understanding of the vocabulary, see
John 6:56, where the one who "remains" or "abides" in Jesus is
the one who eats his flesh and drinks his blood. "Remaining"
in Jesus leads, therefore, to a communion of life. See also John

14:10, where the Father "remains" in Jesus and becomes the source of his actions, which indicates the closest possible union between two persons. In John 15:9 the concept is explicit: The "remaining" of the faithful in Christ is a union of love, and the love of Jesus for those who are his is like the love of the Father for him.

So our "remaining" in Christ brings us, through him, into the secret of the inter-Trinitarian life, the union which binds the Father to the Son, because we are in Christ and Christ is in the Father, and the Father is with the Son, and in the person of the Son we meet the Father. "Remaining in love" is explained on the level of practical realization: It is manifested in carrying out the will of the beloved.

The life which the Christian receives by remaining united to Jesus is manifested in "fruit," that is, in the actions being done for the glory of the Father, the vinegrower, who does all the caring for the vine. It is impossible for the branch to bear fruit if it is cut off from the plant: "without me you can do nothing." The doctrine is found already in 1 Corinthians 12:1ff. Paul speaks of the different tasks each one of us has in the church, although the animating source is the same God who works in all. Each of us, as a member of the church, has his or her own particular function, as in the human body, one organism endowed with one life, each part has its own task. This establishes a solidarity among the members through which the action of one has repercussions on the others (v. 26).

This variety of tasks among the members of the body of Christ — the body which is in the process of being built up — leads us to "grow up in every way into him who is the head" (Ephesians 4:11, 15). The body of Christ is not a static reality; it is not completely finished. Rather, it is being built through the collaboration of humanity with the action of God and will be completed only when "God will be all in all." In the body of Christ, each one carries out his or her own particular work, but it is carried out "in him," that is, united to Christ, who is the source of the unity among the members.

In the First Letter of Peter (2:4ff), a different comparison is used to illustrate the same truth: Jesus is a "living stone," and thus Christians are "living stones" that are used to build a spiritual temple. The temple is the place of worship for the glory of the Father. This clarifies the purpose of the building up of the body of Christ. The image of the stone is completed with Ephesians 2:11ff., where, always in reference to Jesus as the source of unity, Jesus is specified as the "cornerstone" of the building, the stone without which the building could not exist and in which the building finds its connection so as to be able to "grow into a holy temple in the Lord."

We find another image in relation to the same doctrine outside sacred scripture. The image is in a letter to the Ephesians from St. Ignatius, bishop of Antioch, a disciple of the apostles who was martyred in Rome at the beginning of the second century. St. Ignatius uses the image of a chorus in which each of us, "taking the tone from God," sings "in the harmony of concord with one voice, in unison, through the mouth of Jesus Christ to the Father; and he will listen to you, and by your good works he will know that you are members of his Son." The image is different, but the doctrine is the same: The one who brings the songs of everyone together is the "mouth" of Christ who — here as well — is the means by which our praise reaches the Father.

Every image we have examined presents fundamentally the same doctrine, yet each one has a particular aspect that helps us to form a complete idea, as far as is possible, of the reality of the presence of God's life in us and the effects of that presence. The idea common to them all is the vital necessity of being united to Jesus. Such a union leads us to a communion of life with God (true vine). The image of the true vine also makes it clear that the union of the believer with Christ brings union with our brothers and sisters, since I cannot be part of a plant without being united to its branches also. There is, then, a union we could call vertical, by which Christ links us to the Father, and a horizontal union that, always in Christ, links us to our brothers and sisters.

From one point of view or the other, the connecting point of relationship, the vital trunk of the plant, is always Christ. Here we could formulate one of the basic liturgical laws: We do not save ourselves by ourselves. There is no salvation without God or without our brothers and sisters, because more than saving individuals, God wants to establish a kingdom, that is, a community, in which the good of one is the good of all and the evil of one is the evil of all. As Christians, we cannot be indifferent to the salvation of others, because we will be fully saved only when we come into possession of our glorified body, that is, at the moment of parousia; and this will happen when "God will be all in all."

In the kingdom of God, each one of us has our own work to accomplish, not only for our personal advantage but in order to build the whole body of Christ so that it reaches its perfect stature. It is actually a reality in the process of developing. The one who makes the different parts of the body form a single organism is the cornerstone. United to it, the living stones build up that holy temple which represents their objective, because the purpose of the people of God is to give praise to the Father in Christ.

In this fundamental point of the Christian message we have the sublimation of the social interchange among people. Even at the human level, an individual cannot live in isolation; however, the bond among people is a moral, social or spiritual one, a spirit of fellowship that does not go beyond the human plane. When we speak of the people of God, that which unites us with God and with one another is a union that is vital in nature, a real communion of life that we are accustomed to calling "grace," a communion that raises human beings from the human world up to God's world and gives us access into the intimacy of the life of the three divine persons.

The Christological-Trinitarian Structure of Liturgy

AS WE TRY TO INVESTIGATE THE VITAL FUNCTION
of liturgy for the people of God, we begin again with the image
of the body. Just as it is essential for our body to breathe, it
is essential for the body of Christ to perform liturgy. We can
consider liturgy to be the breath of the body of Christ, the
function by which it receives life from God and by which it gives
the praise that is God's due.

Worship, like breathing, comprises two moments: the
first when everything is given to us from on high, the second
when everything returns from humanity to God. This is the
dynamism by which the Mystical Body lives. Accordingly, liturgy
can be understood as an exchange between heaven and earth
and between earth and heaven, heaven sending its gifts to earth
and earth, as far as it is able, responding and reciprocating
the gifts from heaven through Christ and the Spirit's operative
and animating presence.

Here we must pause to consider something of primary
importance. When I said "God," I implicitly affirmed the
great mystery of our religion: unity and trinity. Recall that we
understand mystery to mean something that belongs to God,
something that is hidden in God and which God's goodness has
made known to humanity.

The Old Testament revealed God as the one God. The
New Testament revealed to humanity that God is triune. There
are two terms in this truth: unity and trinity. I may give one
or the other first place, not by attributing greater actual importance to one but only by giving greater attention to one or to
the other from my own subjective point of view. In this sense I
can begin by focusing on the unity of God's nature in such a
way that it comes to the foreground of my attention, and then,
in a second moment, come to consider the distinction of
the persons in the Trinity. In doing so, even though there is no

affirmation of a doctrinal nature being made of the preeminence of one of these elements over the other, the major focus of our attention is in fact the unity of God.

This focus on the unity of God has been the prevailing way of approaching the trinitarian mystery in Western theology since Augustine; after Thomas Aquinas and the scholastics it became the exclusive way. This method, in itself permissible and perfectly orthodox, eventually brought about the result in some cases that the other aspect of God, while not forgotten, was nonetheless overshadowed: namely, the New Testament revelation of the knowledge of another secret of God, the Trinity.

Scripture, and consequently liturgy, followed a different path. Scripture offers a close-up of the Trinity, of really distinct persons, presenting what each one does on behalf of humanity and presupposing the uniqueness of the nature of the three persons. Merely leafing through the Gospel of John one will notice how the distinction of the persons is put into such clear relief (John 14:16 – 26; 16:7ff.)

This second way of looking at the mystery of the Trinity offers the advantage of focusing on the new element revealed in the New Testament. Besides introducing us to the three persons through the specific deeds each performs on behalf of humanity, it adds to our knowledge an aspect of God that is more concrete and closer to our human life. With this method we do not reflect so much on God as a cold abstraction, which can lead to a sense of the insurmountable distance between us and God. Rather, through this approach we come to know God at work, particularly in the magnificent deeds God works in each one of us.

As we said, this is the method of scripture whereby God's self-communication is made known to us through the events in the history of salvation, whereas the other method we mentioned shows traces of the influence of Greek philosophy, which proceeds by abstractions. We will follow the method of scripture and reflect on the function that each person of the Trinity performs in the work of our sanctification, which comes about through the worship we define as the "breathing" of the body of Christ.

The Father is the source of everything: "Every generous act of giving, with every perfect gift, is from above, coming down from the Father of lights" (James 1:17). The Father is the alpha and the omega: In the history of salvation, he is the creator and the end of everything, since the history of salvation prepares the moment when "God will be all in all" and Christ will hand back the transformed world to the Father.

We know already that the mediator of every gift from the Father is Jesus (see in particular the priestly discourse of Jesus, John 17:1ff.), that is, the incarnate Son who is in a position to unite humanity to the Father precisely because Christ assumed our human nature. The sanctifier is the Holy Spirit, whose name comes from precisely that function. The Holy Spirit makes the Father's gifts alive, efficacious and efficient in each one of us, gifts of the Father which, however, come to us solely through Jesus, who is the "way" to the Father, the "gate of the sheepfold." If we recall the image of the true vine, we can say that the life of the plant comes from the Father, that it reaches the branches obviously by passing through the true vine who is Jesus, and that it is the Holy Spirit who makes the sap in the branches full of life and life-giving. This three-fold work carried out in us is the seal of the Holy Trinity on each one of us.

Thus, everything comes from the Father through the mediation of the Son, in the operative presence of the Holy Spirit. This is the moment liturgists call "coming forth from God" (*exitus a Deo*), when God appears as the source of all things, that is, *alpha*. Yet God is also *omega*, the end to which all things are directed. This is the second moment of encounter, when the creature, having received everything from the Father, gives the Father praise for his greatness and for the gifts received. This second moment unfolds in the same way as the first: We have received, through the humanity of Jesus, the Holy Spirit, who sanctifies us. Once sanctified, we are capable of giving praise to the Father. But our praise cannot reach the Father except through the Son and with the Holy Spirit giving it life. Corresponding to the *exitus* is the "return to God" *(reditus ad Deum)*.

Liturgists synthesize this structure of worship with this formula: from – through – in – to, which means from the Father *(a Patre)*, through the Son *(per Filium)*, in the Spirit *(in Spiritu Sancto)*, and through the Son to the Father *(ad Patrem)*. This structure is still evident today, for example, in the conclusion of the Roman Canon and other eucharistic prayers:

Through Christ our Lord
you give us all these gifts.
You fill them with life and goodness,
you bless them and make them holy
[all comes from the Father through Christ].

Through him, with him, in him,
in the unity of the Holy Spirit
all glory and honor is yours, almighty Father,
forever and ever.

Everything returns to the Father always through Christ, in the operative presence of the Holy Spirit.

Ways of Living Liturgy: Prayer

LITURGY, WHICH WE DEFINED AS A SORT OF "breathing" of the body of Christ, uses certain means by which the Father's gift reaches humanity and humanity gives to the Father the honor and love that is his due: These means are prayer and the sacraments.

We are used to thinking about prayer especially in terms of what we might call the *human part in prayer,* which is actually the second moment of prayer, when the person responds to God. In liturgy, as in life, there is always, as we have seen, a twofold movement: from above to below and from below to above. The descending movement always comes first, because its origin is in God, the source of everything. Prayer is the response to the One who speaks to us first. Prayer is listening to the One who has spoken before we do, to the One who calls each of us by name. Above all, prayer is receiving God's gift. The psalmist says: "O Lord, open my lips, and my mouth will declare your praise" (Psalm 51:15).

In prayer, too, the Father's gift comes through Jesus, and, always through his mediation, the praise of God's creatures rises to the Father while the heavenly gift and the person's word are vivified by the Holy Spirit. If we examine prayer primarily in its first phase or *moment* — the descent from the Father to humanity — we will understand how prayer is always valid and effective in whatever form it is expressed.

Prayer is our acceptance of the vital "sap" the Father sends us through Christ the "true vine." Prayer is always an enrichment, whether or not we obtain whatever it is asking for in particular, since it is always contact with God. Prayer is not oriented toward exerting an action on God so that God will lavish grace on us. Rather, prayer is inclined to exert an action primarily on the person who prays so that he or she might receive the Father's grace.

Prayer is first of all a state of being before it is an act; it is above all an attitude of openness, desire and acceptance. When prayer becomes word, it is expressed in various forms. The "Our Father," which Jesus taught us, is petitionary prayer. The first part is especially a petition for the general needs of the king-dom of God, an invocation for its fulfillment. Therefore it is charged with eschatological tension. Nonetheless, eschatology is built already within the hearts and actions of humanity right now, so that in the second part, the "Our Father" expresses requests which deal with our present situation and needs.

Without doubt, Jesus insisted on petitionary prayer. Petition expresses a desire, and desire is the wealth of the poor. This form of prayer makes us conscious of our poverty, aware that we are not yet saved except in hope. However, this poverty is placed into the hands of God, with whom is all fullness. Jesus taught us how and when to pray in petition. In the parable of the insistent friend (Luke 11:5ff.), the man goes to ask help of his friend on behalf of the person who has arrived at his house, because he himself is in no way able to provide for the traveler's needs. Even more, he asks insistently and with confident trust. Nonetheless, the focal point of the parable is the "three loaves of bread" and the meaning they contain. They are loaves to satisfy a friend's hunger, but also and primarily they are the Holy Spirit, whom God "gives to those who ask him" (see Luke 11:13ff.). What is important to highlight in the parable is that the friend who welcomes the guest "has nothing"; his hands are empty. It is when we can do nothing that it is just and proper to ask.

Another form of prayer is thanksgiving, which expresses an awareness of the gifts received and recognizes God as their source.

Finally, in the prayer of Jesus there is the prayer of praise: "I thank you, Father, Lord of heaven and earth, because you have hidden these things from the wise and the intelligent and have revealed them to infants" (Matthew 11:25). Praise expresses an interior movement that introduces nuances that are different from the prayer of thanksgiving. In the prayer of thanksgiving, one begins with the enjoyment of a gift in order to rise up to God. Whereas prayer of praise first springs forth from the contemplation of God's presence and goodness, a second moment reveals these divine attributes in God's works.

Prayer of praise is like a cry of wonder and astonishment in the face of a magnificent reality; it is the expression of enthusiasm in the presence of the greatness of God. Prayer of praise is truly an *elevation* of the soul, which is then made concrete in the contemplation of a specific work of God: "Blessed be the Lord God of Israel, for he has looked favorably on his people and redeemed them" (Luke 1:68). The why comes after: in the first moment one's gaze is turned to God, without realizing, as it were, that God works these great deeds on our behalf and for our good (C. Di Sante, *La preghiera d'Israele* [Marietti: 1985], passim.). Prayer of praise does not begin with the benefit received. Instead, the one who prays fastens on the person of God and is enchanted by God's goodness and greatness. "Give thanks to him, bless his name. For the LORD is good; his steadfast love endures forever" (Psalm 100:4, 5). Praise is a form of prayer frequently found in the Old Testament and in the Jewish liturgical tradition (where it is called *berakhah*).

Sacraments

AND THE WORD BECAME FLESH

AND LIVED AMONG US,

AND WE HAVE SEEN HIS GLORY,

THE GLORY AS OF A FATHER'S ONLY SON,

FULL OF GRACE AND TRUTH.

JOHN 1:14

The Means of the Liturgy:
Sacraments as Perceptible Signs

IN THE SACRAMENTS, THE ENCOUNTER WITH GOD
is made concrete not only in words but also in perceptible
or tangible elements (water, bread, wine, and so on). The entire
Bible could be defined as the history of encounter between
humanity and God. It is an ongoing, progressive encounter, yet
it is never perfect due to the fact that God's faithful giving is
not met with a correspondingly faithful response on the part of
the human creature. When God makes a covenant with a person,
it is always a gift gratuitously offered, a gift that calls forth a
response, a commitment on our part. Yet while God is always
faithful in giving us gifts, the same cannot always be said of our
response. Therefore, the Bible can be thought of as the history
of God's constant call to humanity and of our inconstant and
imperfect response.

The perfect encounter occurs only in Jesus, who is
Son of God and, as such, manifests, in his being human, God's
love for all humanity. Jesus is the greatest gift from the Father
to sanctify us: As Son of the Father, Jesus manifests his coming
from the Father *(exitus a Deo)*. But Jesus is also a human being,
and as such he is the greatest manifestation of human love
for God — the best, most perfect expression of this love. Jesus
achieves in himself the highest homage one can give to the
Father. His human life is the greatest praise that can rise from
earth to heaven. In the person of Christ, then, we find also the
return to the Father *(reditus ad Patrem)*. In the humanity of
Jesus, the meeting between God and humanity — God's gift and
our response — is perfect. This perfect encounter is meant to
spread and to fill the whole of creation with its fullness.

If this quality of encounter is accomplished in the human body of Christ, it must extend in a particular way to the body that is his people. But if the perfect encounter in Christ took place in the materiality of a human body, then the encounter that extends to his people must take place through a concrete material element as well.

Therefore, the first reason for the presence of a perceptible element in the sacraments will be found in the incarnation, the determining event in the entire history of salvation. Christianity, before it is a system of thought, before it is a particular morality, is an event: the incarnation of the Son of God, the manifestation of God in matter, in the concreteness of a human body. The relationship of each of us with God is conditioned by this fact. In the relationship of each one of us with God we will find the reflection of this fundamental fact: The divine is always manifested through the tangible and the human. We call this "the law of the incarnation."

We come across this law again and again throughout the history of salvation. Creation is the first manifestation of God, and in it God is manifested in rocks, in the expanse of seas and in other displays. God's self-revelation to Moses was seen in the fire that burned but was not consumed, and so on. Manifestations by means of perceptible elements are always what reveal the presence of God, but since they are different from God, at the same time they hide God's presence.

The same thing happens in the greatest manifestation of God in the tangible, in matter: the incarnation. The human body of Christ reveals and at the same time conceals God: "He is the son of a carpenter" said some. "You are the son of the living God," affirms Peter. There were those who saw only a man in Christ and others who, through a special revelation from the Father, managed to look beyond appearances and to adore God in the body of this man. It is the scandal of the incarnation, a scandal that consists exactly in the fact that God's self-revelation is linked to elements of such scant importance.

THE SCANDAL OF THE INCARNATION

The *scandal of the incarnation,* which began at creation, is present
in all history and emerges particularly in certain events: For
example, God's self-manifestation is connected in a special way
to the history of one people, the Jews. It is continued in the
church, where the encounter with God takes place by means of
sacraments that are "perceptible signs" in which a material
and perceptible element is always present. It is hard to believe
that the salvific action of Christ can be tied to a drop of water,
his presence to bread and wine. It is even more scandalous that
the gift of God is effected through human beings, who are
not always worthy vehicles.

　　And yet, there is no baptism without water; there is no
eucharist without bread and wine. Without the minister and
community, there is no sacrament. Water, bread, wine and other
tangible elements are actually visible and efficacious signs of
an invisible reality that cannot be perceived by the senses.
In current usage, sign is not clearly distinguished from *symbol,*
and the use of the two terms fluctuates in the language of
liturgists themselves. The Second Vatican Council pointed out
that "in the liturgy the sanctification of men and women is
given expression in symbols perceptible by the senses and is
carried out in ways appropriate to each of them" (*Constitution
on the Sacred Liturgy,* 7).

SIGNIFIER AND SIGNIFIED

Whether we use sign or symbol, we mean to indicate a perceptible element — that is, visible and tangible — which contains
in itself and expresses a reality different from itself. On the
subject of sign, Augustine said: "One thing is seen, another is
understood" *(Aliud videtur, aliud intelligitur).* In signs there
is a *signifier,* consisting of the perceptible element, and a *signified,*
consisting of the reality beyond the perceptible to which we
are recalled. Precisely because it is beyond the capacity of the
senses to perceive, it would not be possible to apprehend or

reach that reality if we did not find support in the visible and tangible element.

The two elements of the sign are closely interconnected, that is, we cannot think of signifier as a cloak wrapping the outside of the signified. Chenu says: "The symbol is not an accessory, an adornment of the mystery, nor a provisional pedagogy; it is the coessential resource of its communication."[1]

We have referred to the *scandal* of the necessary presence of material elements in the liturgy, the most particular means of the encounter with God. It is a question of a scandal that we cannot avoid by escaping into a disembodied spiritualism. If we lose sight of the *signifier,* we lose the *signified* as well, since they are indissolubly united. If we lose sight of the human body of Christ, we lose the mystery of the incarnation. The sign is simultaneously the same as and distinct from the thing that is signified. Modern mentality has taken to seeing the difference instead, thereby making the sign something lacking true reality. We must instead understand that signs are the reality they indicate, realities that we would be unable to reach if their material element did not both reveal and veil them.

TYPES OF SIGNS

There are various types of signs. There are creation-signs, which culminate in the human person, the image of God, and above all, in Christ, the greatest manifestation of the transcendent God. Event-signs are occurrences that reveal God's care in guiding history in every moment. Among these, the Exodus stands out in the Jewish tradition; in the Christian tradition, the incarnation. There are also the ritual-signs that make up the liturgy itself, and in the *memorial* they actualize the event-signs.

Among the various signs, particular importance is attributed to the word. The word is a sign that, because it consists of sounds and therefore of something perceptible, is used to express a thought, an intent, that one could not other-wise perceive. The word-sign has a special importance in liturgy, since it is the tangible manifestation of the will of God and the church. It is the will of God that determines the worth of the tangible element in the sacraments and directs it toward a specific purpose. For example, in baptism and confirmation the element of oil is the same, but the difference in the words spoken over the oil in the two sacraments, and thus the distinct will of God, makes the oil have an effect that is different in confirmation than it is in baptism.

Then there are sign-gestures, the most frequent of which is the sign of the cross (to which we will return later). Genuflecting belongs to the category of signs that express sentiment, a state of spirit, and at the same time invigorate us by engaging the whole body. The signs tend toward a complete attuning of one's whole person to the liturgical reality, because the whole of one's body is involved in it. Saint Augustine calls gestures "sensible words" and, indeed, to genuflect or to say "I feel small before God" are in fact the same thing.

Additionally, we have sign-objects, to which, for example, liturgical colors belong, or sign-environments, such as the darkened church at Easter that is meant to express the temporary triumph of evil while the light (the lit candles) expresses the resurrection, the return of life, the triumph over evil. A most special place is reserved in the liturgy for sign-persons. At the eucharist, the Christian community points to that intangible, invisible reality of the body of Christ that gives honor to the Father, while the various tasks of the participants at Mass (celebrant, lector, those who bring the gifts to the altar, and so on) reflect the diversity of duties of the members of the body of Christ.

LITURGICAL SIGNS

Liturgical signs present four features that we will find in the majority of the sacraments, all of which we must consider in relation to the person of Christ, who is *the* celebrant of the sacraments.

First, liturgical signs are above all *rememorative* of the salvific actions accomplished by Christ. For example, in the ancient baptismal liturgy, going down into the baptismal pool was the remembrance and in some way the reproducing of Jesus' descent into the tomb, while coming out of the water was the remembrance and repetition of the resurrection. The very time at which baptism was conferred was *rememorative,* since in the first centuries baptism was celebrated mainly at Easter, on the night when Jesus passed from death to life.

Second, liturgical signs are *demonstrative* of the action Christ is working in us, of the supernatural, invisible reality that they produce: the flow of grace into us and praise rising up to the Father. They make us *see* what the sacrament is doing. Thus, for example, the baptismal water indicates — and actuates — the washing away of all sin and the giving of life. The words of the rite are both the proclamation of salvation for the believers and an act of faith in God on the part of the believer.

Third, liturgical signs are *binding* on the moral conduct of the believer. That is, they express the commitment the person takes on as a response to God's gift, as, for instance, in renouncing Satan in baptism.

Finally, we know that the kingdom of heaven, inaugurated by Jesus and in which we participate by means of the sacraments, is a reality in progress that nonetheless anticipates and prepares for the final moment in salvation history. Consequently, liturgical signs are also *prophetic* of the heavenly glory and of Christ's coming in glory. Christ is already present in these signs — in his salvific power and in his very person. Therefore, these signs are already the accomplishment of Christ's coming; the coming, however, is being actualized *under a veil,* that is, in a way that is still incomplete in the human creature although it anticipates and prepares for that future coming when "God will be all in all." In liturgy, then, we are living in a particular way in which Christianity is both *the already and the not yet.*

In closing, we ought not think that the use of signs characterizes only the religious life, although it is there that signs achieve a special intensity. In our own age, it is becoming increasingly clearer that symbolic activity is "a moment of full realization of the human being in his openness to the transcendent and in his social dimension."[2] Sign-symbols are essential tools of communication.

Sacraments and the Subhuman World

AS WE HAVE SEEN, THE ENCOUNTER WITH GOD IN prayer is accomplished essentially through the word. In the sacraments, the encounter with God — God's gift to us and our response in faith and love — also takes place in the perceptible element, present in each one of us. That is to say, in the sacraments we will always find an element from the material world that becomes an instrument in the relationship with God. We know that the subhuman world was made by God for the service of humanity. According to Genesis 1, man and woman received the command from God to dominate and subdue the world around them. They are to realize this dominion through their own work, by means of which the world will be fulfilled and perfected.

However, sin intervenes and causes a break in the harmony between the human creature and God. It interrupts that familiarity that existed between God and his still-innocent creatures. The consequences of sin even go beyond the human world in that the human person is somehow the *mediator* between God and the subhuman world. He is *adam* (human) taken from the *adamah* (earth) and thus an earthly creature

(Genesis 2:7) who at the same time is a bearer of the image of God (Genesis 1:26ff.). When a disorder takes place in the human creature, who stands between God and inanimate matter, such a disorder has to be reflected in matter too.

Sin distances the person from God, and the person from the inferior world as well. Because of sin, the lower level of life becomes diverted from its aim, which is to serve humanity, just as by sinning, human creatures are diverted from the service of God, which is their end. The human creature, the reigning creature of nature, puts its own imprint on nature, whether in the positive sense — as happened before sin, when nature was submissive — or in the negative sense: To the one who sins there corresponds a nature that rebels. And so the world becomes hostile to the human creature. The command to "till and keep" the world (Genesis 2:15), and hence to subdue and rule it, still exists, but now this stewardship is exercised over a rebellious nature which will produce "thorns and thistles" and will force man and woman to draw sustenance from the earth by the sweat of their face (Genesis 3:19). The world becomes at times a tool of punishment from God: The Lord will command the clouds not to rain on his much-loved vineyard because it has brought forth sour grapes (Isaiah 5).

Nature suffers from this state of being and is waiting to be freed from the disorder into which the human creature has led it (Romans 8:18ff.). Creation is waiting to be set free by the "children of God," by those who will have restored the image of God within themselves and thus will put on the created world of nature the positive imprint that Adam could have made before sin. These renewed human beings will bring about the fulfillment of the prophecy that speaks of a "new heaven and a new earth," because being renewed, they will make a new imprint on nature, including their own bodies, and at that time the human body will be filled with the resurrection.

JESUS: LINK BETWEEN THE HUMAN WORLD
AND SUBHUMAN WORLD

Yet what humanity awaits at the end of time has already
happened in Jesus the man. Things have already been changed
with the Incarnation. In the human body of Christ, a new
solidarity between the human and subhuman world has been
established, no longer a solidarity in disorder and rebellion but in
harmony and obedience. In the human body of Christ, nature
reaches the summit of union with God, renders the greatest
possible service to God and becomes the most docile instrument
of the divinity. In Jesus the man, the harmony that existed
between the human and subhuman world before sin is restored.
This harmony, effected in his own person, radiates from and
around Jesus: Waves are calmed at the sound of his voice; fero-
cious animals become tame before him. Jesus rules the elements
of nature perfectly and peacefully, and uses them in a natural way.

We know how the Incarnation places an imprint on
the whole of past history, which converges in it, and on the
whole of future history, which draws its life-giving impulse from
it. We know how liturgy springs from the incarnation just as
effect flows from cause. Accordingly, in liturgy that same
submission of the material world to the human creature must
be found as it occurred in the person of Jesus. In liturgy the
material world must re-enter the order willed for it by God; it
must put itself back in service to the human creature in
complete docility. In fact, in liturgy the subhuman world gives
the ultimate service to us by becoming the instrument of
our encounter with God: Water is the necessary instrument for
entrance into the church, oil is used to confirm the image of
Christ in us, and finally, in the eucharist we have the most
extraordinary inclusion, elevation and transfiguration of the
material world in service of the divine life.

Here is how Vagaggini puts it in the first volume of his
work *The Theological Dimensions of the Liturgy:*

Aside from the assumption of a human body by the Son of God, there is no more wonderful example of the importance of the role played by this material world in the divine plan.

The bread and the wine, whose whole substance is changed into the substance of Christ's body and blood, serve as a substratum or a vehicle for the real presence of Christ. Thus they are intimately associated to that whole current of divine life for humanity, of joy for the angels and the saints, and of glory for God, which is the effect of the eucharistic sacrifice. Thus the Mass realizes, as perfectly as possible before the time of the new heaven and the new earth, the redemption of material creation, that liberation from the slavery of sin and corruption of which Saint Paul speaks.[3]

Liturgy as the actualization of the salvific act of Christ and its personal application is already an anticipation of the future world. We know that Jesus, the perfect person, anticipates the perfect humanity of the parousia. Therefore, by participating in the sacraments, we anticipate in ourselves the future harmony of the cosmos that we are awaiting at the end of time. We are dealing with a harmony restored *under the veil,* a partial and initial restoration, since it has not yet reached the full extent it will have when "God will be all in all." Sin still reigns in sinners as well as in the just who suffer the consequences of sin, but it is a real and concrete restoration nonetheless.

Sacraments as Acts of Christ

WE HAVE EXAMINED THE SACRAMENTS AS A reflection and consequence of the Incarnation, as those means whose perceptible elements reflect the human body of Christ in our religious life. We have seen how the dissension that separates the human from the subhuman world already is being healed now in the sacraments. What remains is to examine sacraments in terms of the singularity of each of them and in terms of the individuality of the person who receives them.

Redemption gains salvation for us. Ever since the death and resurrection of Christ-made-man, we can say that salvation is made available to humanity. However, "a sacrament is not redemption pure and simple, but rather redemption as directed to a particular human . . . need for it."[4] "A sacrament is essentially Christ's redemptive act being perfected with regard to a particular subject."[5] And: "A sacrament is the sign or the visibility of Jesus' act of redemption considered not in itself but precisely as affecting this particular person."[6]

In the sacraments, Jesus the Savior applies himself personally to the individual believer. Jesus "seizes" the person, Schillebeeckx says so aptly, and communicates divine life to each according to each one's need. To name just a few examples, at baptism the person is given birth into the divine life of Christ; through the sacrament of reconciliation this life is restored by Christ, and Christ nourishes each believer in the eucharist.

The sacraments repeat on the supernatural level the miracles Jesus performed during his earthly life. In the miracles, Jesus' power to heal is applied to individuals. To some he gives back their sight, to others their hearing, to some their very lives, and still others he cures of different illnesses. The same occurs in the sacraments: Redemption is applied to the individual person, but with different operations. When Jesus worked a miracle, he would turn to, talk with, or touch the individual. In the sacraments, Jesus turns to each single believer and, through the minister who is the sign of his presence, makes these gestures, speaks and acts according to his will.

If the sacraments are acts of Christ, can we establish an order of importance among them? The most important act in the life of Christ was the total offering of himself. Jesus' entire life was an offering; it was an offering which culminated, however, with Calvary and the resulting glorification by the

Father. Therefore, first place among the sacraments will belong to the one that actualizes that total offering in a particular way: the eucharist. All the other sacraments are actually ordered in relation to it, and only in it do they derive their full meaning.

Baptism confers on us an initial resemblance to Christ that is perfected in confirmation. This resemblance is intended to lead us to be and act like Jesus, and as such enables us to participate in the act which more than all others expresses the gift of Christ to humanity. Baptism and confirmation grant us the garment for worship, the garment we must wear in order to share in the banquet. The sacraments of reconciliation and, under special conditions, the anointing of the sick restore the garment of worship in its full splendor. The convergence between holy orders and the eucharist is obvious. The priestly ministry — in the Catholic tradition and in many other Christian traditions — is a service rendered to the community especially in relation to the eucharist. Finally, marriage, in that it is a sacrament of union, presents a particular connection with the eucharist, the "sacrament of unity."

Mysterion – Sacramentum

FOR A BETTER UNDERSTANDING OF WHAT A sacrament is, it is timely to explain the meaning of the word. The church first spoke Greek and used the word *mysterion* to say what we now call *sacrament.* This word is found in Paul (Ephesians 1:9), who wanted to indicate by it the free and loving plan of God — known only to God — for the salvation of humanity and revealed to us at a given moment. Thus, *mysterion* for Paul is something hidden in God and communicated to humanity through God's goodness.

In the works of the Fathers from Origen on, *mysterion* has meant a perceptible thing that contains hidden in itself a divine reality manifested to whomever has the capacity to perceive it. We speak of the *mysterion* of Christ in which the invisible is his own divinity, and the perceptible reality is his humanity. We speak of the *mysterion* of scripture, the word that enables us to know God. Finally, we speak of *mysterion* in relation to the rites of worship that contain the invisible or intangible reality under the veil of visible or perceptible signs. All these meanings we find in the corresponding Latin word: *mysterium*.

The Latin word *sacramentum* was not coined expressly for the Christian sacraments but existed before them, and it is therefore necessary to know the earlier meaning. It was a military term and indicated rites of initiation and consecration to the guardian deities of the army. These rites included an oath of loyalty and hence an obligation on the part of the participant. Tertullian, by carrying the word over into Christian language, emphasized in particular this last element, thereby giving greater importance to the obligation on our part than it had in the word *mysterion*, in which the gift of God is preeminent.

We have here an early expression of Western humanism that put the human moral element in the foreground, as opposed to the Greek, which speaks of a divine reality hidden from and revealed to humanity through a gift of God. Keeping in mind this development of the vocabulary, we can say that sacraments are acts of Christ by which he communicates his divine life to us. This divine life belongs to God. Hidden in God, it is communicated to us through God's goodness. Receiving this gift from God constitutes a commitment for us and asks for a response from us. And since this gift of God is communicated to us in the context of the Christian community, through the mediation of a minister, we can say that sacraments are not only acts of Christ but also acts of the church as well.

The sacraments, we could say also, are an irruption of God into our lives. God comes into our lives and transforms us at the level of being and acting, of acting as a consequence of the transformation effected at the level of being, because by becoming and thus being different, we also act differently. This, then, is our commitment: that we act according to the new ontological level, the level of being where we now find ourselves.

---

1. Cited in *Nuovo Dizionario di Liturgia* (Ed. Paoline, 1983), 1379.

2. *Dizionario liturgico,* 1371.

3. C. Vagaggini, *The Theological Dimension of the Liturgy,* vol. 1., trans. Leonard J. Doyle (Collegeville, MN: The Liturgical Press, 1959), 182.

4. E. Schillebeeckx, OP, *Christ the Sacrament of the Encounter with God* (New York: Sheed and Ward, 1963), 79.

5. Ibid., 80.

6. Ibid., 81.

PART FOUR

Sacraments of Initiation

WHEN YOU WERE BURIED

WITH HIM IN BAPTISM,

YOU WERE ALSO RAISED WITH HIM

THROUGH FAITH IN THE POWER OF GOD,

WHO RAISED HIM FROM THE DEAD.

COLOSSIANS 2:12

Baptism

BAPTISM IS THE SACRAMENT THAT IMPRINTS THE
initial likeness of Christ on the human person; it is the first step
of Christian initiation. To *initiate* means to let someone share
in a life, in this case, the life of the risen Christ. The risen life of
Christ is a transformed and empowered life, since it is totally
permeated with the Holy Spirit; it is the life of Jesus glorified by
the Father after his passion. At baptism, Christians are given
a new life whose source is Christ, the effective cause, model and,
we could say, *reserve;* that is, the new life is found in a concentrated form in the resurrected body of Jesus, and we can draw
new life from this source so as to participate in and enjoy it.

Just as at the center of the history of salvation the cross
of Christ restores what Adam spoiled (he who was defeated
through the wood of the tree of knowledge in Paradise now
becomes victorious through the wood of the cross), so baptism
applies to each person that *healing* the cross obtained. Through
baptism, the central point of salvation history — salvation as
concentrated in the person of Christ — gradually widens, thereby
building the Mystical Body of Christ, always adding new
branches to the true vine, building the spiritual temple for the
praise of the Father.

From baptism is born a kingdom of new persons who
share in a new quality of life: the life of the risen Christ. This
new race is created. As the human race descended from Adam
was created in the beginning by the word of God, so too is
the new human race descended from Christ created by the sacramental act and word, which are Christ's act and word. In
baptism, it is Christ who takes hold of, or *seizes,* the person and
transforms him or her by communicating his own fullness of life.

As the human race has its origin in Adam, so the new human race has its origin in the risen Christ. The resurrection is the great event of the world, compared to which any other historical event pales. The very creation at the beginning of the world loses its importance when seen in the light of the second creation, a creation on a higher plane, a new life, the very life of God. As resurrection is the *second creation,* so baptism is the second birth.

BIRTH INTO A NEW LIFE

At this point we need to reread Jesus' conversation with Nicodemus (John 3:11ff). In it, Jesus is speaking about a birth which he describes with a word *(anothen)* that in Greek means *again* and *from above.* With this single word, the Greek text specifies the particularity of this birth: It is *again,* that is, distinct from physical birth, and it is *from above,* that is, it springs from a higher life source. It is realized "through water and the Holy Spirit." We know that the resurrection of Christ occurs through the Spirit, who is in full possession of Jesus' humanity.

The Christian's new birth is like that of Christ, and thus the instrument will again be the Holy Spirit. As to the "water," we must see the obvious allusion to baptism by water while not forgetting, however, that water and Spirit frequently were associated already in the Old Testament, and often the action of the Spirit is made evident by the fertile action of water. The Spirit vivifies souls as water vivifies bodies. They are both sources of life, although on different levels. Reflecting on the power of one clarifies the power of the other.

The principle of life from which this new birth originates is made clear in verse 15: The Son of Man who will be "lifted up" on the cross and, thus sacrificed, is "lifted up" to the right hand of the Father, that is, glorified. These realities are being fulfilled in turn. Indeed, the purpose of the sacrifice of the Son of Man is to give us eternal life, the life that springs from being born "again" and "from above."

Given that baptism is birth into a new life, we must now clarify how this new life is to be understood. It is defined as "eternal life," which in turn is explained by John (17:3) as to "know you [the Father], the only true God, and Jesus Christ whom you have sent." On this subject, Paul speaks of "illumination," as do the majority of the Fathers of the church. We should see the reflection of this idea in the custom of clothing the baptized child or adult in a white garment and giving to the newly baptized the lighted candle.

The new birth can be understood also as the signing of the image of Christ on the baptized person. The purpose of the Christian life is very precise: to become like Christ, to become the *same* as Christ. Baptism gives us an initial likeness destined to grow in confirmation and, above all, in the eucharist. In fact, the resemblance to Christ must be understood first of all as resemblance to the central act of his life, the paschal mystery of his death and resurrection, which is actualized in the Mass in a particular way.

Therefore, baptism is first and foremost configuration to the death and resurrection of Christ. (On this subject, see Romans 6:3ff.). As the death of Christ is not the end in itself but leads to the resurrection, so our being "baptized in the death of Christ" leads to a *newness* of life. As the first Adam was followed by the new Adam in the history of salvation, so it is with us.

Just as the risen Jesus will never die again, because in his humanity he has a new principle of life, so we too "will live with him" and be like him. In his resurrection, Jesus was the first to receive, in his humanity, the full communication of divine life, and became from then forward the source of divine life for others. This same presentation of baptism as death and resurrection is taken up again by Paul in Colossians 2:12: "When you were buried with him in baptism, you were also raised with him through faith in the power of God, who raised him from the dead." This is the same doctrine we find in Galatians 2:20: "It is no longer I who live, but it is Christ who lives in me." The one who "lives no longer" is the old Adam, the sinner, and the One who "lives in me" is the risen Christ. Cerfaux says: "According to the line of Pauline theology, the power that raised Christ does not stop at him but brings forth life in the Christian, a life that belongs to the same source and nature as that of the risen Christ."[1]

Christ, the center and source of new life, shares that life with all Christians, and therefore baptism brings me into communion of life with Christ and all my brothers and sisters. Baptism gives me birth into the true vine in which I am grafted onto Christ, and thus, by necessity, I encounter those who, like me, compose the branches of the plant. Baptism is both an individual and a communal fact. We know that the Fathers of the church compare baptism to the passage through the Red Sea. The passage through the Red Sea constitutes Israel as a new people: From baptism, new persons are born who make up a new people, the new branch of the people of God.

ANCIENT BAPTISMAL LITURGY

To reconstruct the oldest liturgical baptismal practices, we must go back to the Acts of the Apostles (chapter 2), which has preserved for us the chronicle of the first Christian baptism ever celebrated. We know that it took place on the very day of Pentecost, a most significant connection that makes us understand baptism as participation in the gift of the Holy Spirit, whom the Father sends to us from heaven, due to and as a consequence of Christ's passover *(pasch),* his death and resurrection.

The actual baptism is preceded by Peter's discourse, which is substantially the proclamation *(kerygma)* that Jesus is risen and that he is Christ the Lord, that is, God. It is not a systematic doctrinal instruction but a proclamation of a fact that truly has taken place. This proclamation is accepted by the crowd with faith and in the spirit of repentance (v. 37), after which the conferring of the sacrament happens. All three parts — the proclamation, the acceptance on the part of the person who believes and repents, and the bathing with water — are elements of the sacrament, that is, of the gift of God to which our response corresponds.

The ritual gradually became more organized until it became a well-structured liturgy with the institution of a period of catechumenate. It is extremely difficult to follow the liturgy in its formation because the vast liturgical unity we know today is the result of a fusion of a plurality of liturgical customs. Tracing them here is neither possible nor our purpose. We will indicate only the most significant elements.

First, the role assigned to the word — which in the beginning had the nature we defined as *kerygma* — is later put on two tracks, one dogmatic and the other moral. The first point, always centered on Christ, begins to take on a christological-trinitarian structure which we can reconstruct from the oldest formulae of the Credo and the many baptismal catecheses that have come down to us. As for the moral side, there is a following of the doctrine of the "two ways," which we find in one of the oldest Christian texts dating from between 80 and 150, the *Didache* or *Teaching of the Twelve Apostles*. Drawing in particular on Deuteronomy and other Old Testament passages, the *Didache* says that there are two ways, one of life and one of death; both are described with much advice on the practical aspect of life. Pedagogically, it was very important that the applicant for baptism be given a choice, thereby making an appeal to one's free will and thus requiring a personal commitment freely undertaken.

From the point of view of ritual, we can say that very soon the custom of baptizing at the Easter Vigil became established in order to show that the sacrament is configured to the crucified and risen Christ, and as Jesus passed from death to life during that night, so the baptized person passes from the state of sin, which is like death, to a new life, the very life of the risen Christ.

The catechumen's wait for baptism could last many years, but the final preparation took place during Lent. This began with the candidates, accompanied by their sponsors, presenting themselves to the bishop to make their application. This application was very solemn: The bishop would place his ceremonial chair in the middle of the church and would examine the candidates, asking their sponsors if they were worthy. This was done out of respect for both the sacrament and the community itself; that is, it emphasized the communal character of baptism, since admitting an unworthy member into the community would have done injury to all. During the forty days of Lent, one entered into the heart of the immediate preparation, comprising complete and proper instruction and rites. The instruction itself was never academic; instead, it was ritual in nature. The bishops taught in such a way that the instruction was not a lesson but, according to the spirit of ancient practice, the solemn proclamation of the salvation in which the catechumens would share at baptism.

Moreover, various rites were performed on the candidates, through which they would begin already to live a real and true religious life, though in an initial way. The main rites that preceded baptism included insufflation, the act of breathing on the person to be baptized. This is explained as a gesture of contempt for the devil, that is, an exorcism, or as the bestowing of the animation of the new Adam, done in imitation of God's breath in the garden of Eden. Another rite was the imposition of the hands, sign of the gift of the Holy Spirit, the *consignatio,* that is, the making of the sign of the cross on the baptized person. The Fathers explained that this sign was like the brand put on the sheep of the Good Shepherd to keep the "wolf" who tries to lay a trap for the flock at bay, and like the soldier's tattoo that indicates the captain he served. The tasting of salt, which in some places took the form of a proper catechumenal meal, signifying a preparation for the eucharistic banquet, was another ritual element of preparation for baptism.

During the lenten period, the catechumens were subjected to scrutinies, and those who failed were not baptized on Easter but had to be examined again and could eventually be baptized on Pentecost. The catechumens were also given the symbol, that is, the Creed, and the ceremony was called *traditio symboli*. After a certain number of days, there was the *redditio symboli*, when the candidates had to show that they had learned it. In some places they used to recite the gospel, the Our Father and sometimes the psalms with great solemnity.

All this took place during the forty days of Lent, at the end of which, on Saturday morning, there was the final exorcism. This exorcism had an obvious symbolism: The catechumens, standing on a hair shirt, were made to face west (the region where the sun sets, a place of darkness and associated with evil). The hair shirt was linked to the garments made from skins that Adam and Eve covered themselves with after the first sin; this signified the desire to trample on that garment and the desire to wipe out sin.

The anointings also had the character of an exorcism. Hippolytus (beginning of the third century) already mentions a prebaptismal anointing, and this is attested to in the Eastern Church around this same period as well. This anointing "was intended to symbolize the [baptized person's] escape from the enemy's grasp, just as the athlete in readiness to enter into the arena to combat the enemy."[2] The post-baptismal anointing is to signify the effects of grace in the neophyte, who thereby becomes the "good fragrance of Christ." This recalls the practice recorded in the Old Testament of anointing priests and kings; this practice prefigured Christ's anointing through which each Christian enters into a "royal priesthood" and "a holy people."

On Saturday night, the catechumens, now turned toward the east, made a threefold profession of faith in God which corresponded to the threefold renunciation of Satan. Finally, the catechumens went down into the baptismal pool, which was considered both the tomb of the old person and the motherly womb of the church, which gave birth to the new person. Going into the pool was like going down into the tomb, and coming up out of the pool was the return to a new life, the life of the risen Christ. To symbolize this transformation and the being set aflame by the radiance of grace, the old garment was removed and the baptized person was clothed in a white garment. They used to crown the baptized as an acknowledgment of the royal dignity which baptism confers, and soon they added the custom of giving a lighted candle.

When the rite of baptism was over, the new Christians went through the *consignatorium,* in which they were confirmed; that is, they received confirmation as the completion of initiation. Finally, dressed in the white garment, they entered the church where the community was gathered, and the community welcomed them in their midst. Together with them, the new Christians took part for the first time in the eucharistic banquet. The white garment, received after the immersion in the baptismal pool, was the gown of worship necessary to take part in the banquet, the garment that the guests invited to the wedding of the king's son were supposed to wear (Matthew 22:1ff.).

The type of place designated for the baptismal ceremony varied with the Jewish Christians and those of other ethnic origins. With the former, a part of their rites would take place in dark caverns, almost "serpent holes"; there they would remove their old garments and, facing west, renounce Satan. Then they would move on to the "caves blazing with light," singing hymns to Christ-Day and repeating "the Lord is my light." Ethnic Christians built baptistries, buildings apart from the church, most often in the shape of an octagon. The number eight had a symbolic meaning: The earth, from its beginning to redemption, had lived the seventh day of creation. From redemption onward, the eighth day began, the time of the new world inhabited by a new humanity. This new time began with the resurrection of Christ, which happened, according to the Jewish calendar in which the Sabbath is the seventh day, on the eighth day of the week. Hence, eight became a number symbolic of Christ.

Confirmation

BAPTISM AND CONFIRMATION ARE SO INTIMATELY related that it is impossible to examine the one without the other. In fact, in ancient liturgy confirmation followed imme-diately after baptism, and both preceded the eucharist. All of this took place in a paschal context, thus making obvious the Christian's assuming the form of the person of Christ, who died and is risen. We must, however, speak of two sacraments of initiation that are clearly distinct from each other: Christian initiation is completed by two successive rites which — even today in the Latin Church — are conferred by different ministers.[3]

   In order to understand the difference in nature and effect between the two sacraments of initiation, we need to consider them each in light of the other. Baptism is the first participation in the life of the risen Christ. Baptism represents in the life of the faithful the moment when the new shoot first appears on the true vine (this is why the newly baptized were called *neophytes,* that is, "newly planted") and the sap of divine life begins to flow in it. Baptism is the first sacrament of Christian initiation, followed by the second, confirmation. If baptism is birth into the Christian life, confirmation is entrance into the age of adulthood and maturity. The likeness to Christ which baptism has given us in an initial form will be perfected in confirmation by completing the transformation baptism had already effected.

We can also say that if baptism produces an internal illumination, confirmation changes it into a beacon's light. If baptism lights a lamp within us, with confirmation this lamp is lifted up onto a lampstool, that is, put to the benefit of the community. If baptism is something the faithful come to enjoy in a rather passive manner, confirmation arms us for battle. If we return to the comparison with natural life, we will see that whereas adults are called to carry out their work in society, children are in a phase of preparation in view of the duties of adult life. In the same way, confirmed Christians must not keep the light closed in within themselves; rather, it is to be placed at the service of others.

Confirmation confers new capabilities that qualify one for action on behalf of the community; we could say that it bestows an opening toward the world which the baptized do not yet have. This effect is indicated by the very material of the sacrament: the chrism, a mixture of oil and balsam, both diffusive by their nature. The oil spreads on the skin and the perfume permeates the air. Confirmation gives the virtue or power of fortitude *(virtus fortitudinis)* in that it strengthens the spirit of believers in order to make them capable of new tasks. Saint Thomas says: "The perfection worked by confirmation is in view of standing firm in oneself" *(Perfectio confirmationis est ad standum fortiter in se ipsum)*. The Holy Spirit has been given to us at confirmation in great abundance for strength *(ad robur)*, for support. Saint Cyril clarifies for us how radical this transformation is that the Holy Spirit effects:

> For just as the one immersed in the waters in baptism is completely encompassed by the water, so they too were completely baptized by the Spirit. The water encompasses the body externally, but the Holy Spirit baptizes the soul perfectly within. Why do you wonder? Take an example from matter. . . . If fire, penetrating the mass of iron, sets the whole aflame, and what was cold becomes hot, and what was

black becomes bright — if the body of fire penetrates the body of iron, why do you wonder, if the Holy Spirit enters the inmost parts of the soul?[4]

Specifying more clearly the transformation effected by confirmation, we could say that we are dealing with a transformation on the level of being (ontological) through which what was spiritually a Christian child becomes spiritually a Christian adult. It is in this sense that we speak of the *perfect* Christian: The child, even at the natural level, is not a "perfect" being, that is, complete, because the child is a being in formation who is aiming toward "perfect" adulthood. We can say the same of the baptized person awaiting confirmation: One still awaits that transformation (that is called *character*) which will make one an ontologically perfect Christian.

Does the sacrament also effect a transformation at the level of doing? We would have to say yes, inasmuch as doing is tied to being. But we would also have to say no, since I could develop as an adult at the level of being and continue to act like a child or like a delinquent. Thus, I answer "yes" to the above question, in the measure that I knowingly accept and consent to this transformative process of becoming an adult. I answer no if my becoming adult happens immediately by my own effort without an informed adherence of the will, that is, if I think it is automatic or instantaneous and that it happens without an interior adhesion.

We mentioned that confirmation completes the likeness to Christ in the Christian; I can be like a certain person; my resemblance to that person can be an ontological reality without affecting my conduct. Or, I can bear the external likeness of a person, and at the same time I can also try to imitate even their manner of acting. In this case it would be a resemblance in the order of being and doing.

THE BAPTISM OF JESUS,
PENTECOST AND CONFIRMATION

The name *Christian* comes from Christ. The resemblance in the name is the reflection of the resemblance that binds the believer to Christ. This is how Saint Cyril, bishop of Jerusalem (fourth century) expressed himself on this subject:

> Baptized into Christ and "clothed with Christ" you have been shaped to the likeness of the Son of God. For God, in "predestining us to be adopted as his children," has "conformed us to the glorified body of Christ." As "partakers of Christ," therefore, you are rightly called "Christs," i.e., "anointed ones"; it was of you that God said: "Touch not my [Christus] Christs." Now, you became Christs by receiving the seal of the Holy Spirit; everything has been wrought in you "likewise" because you are likenesses of Christ. He bathed in the river Jordan and after imparting the fragrance of his Godhead to the waters, came up from them. Him the Holy Spirit visited in essential presence, like resting upon like. Similarly for you, after you had ascended from the sacred streams, there was an anointing with chrism, the seal of that with the Holy Spirit."[5]

The ontological likeness between Christ and his faithful allows us to establish a parallel between the events of the life of Christ and the sacramental life of the Christian. Saint Cyril compares Jesus' baptism in the Jordan to confirmation and points out that the two events have similar effects:

> For as Christ after his baptism and the visitation of the Holy Spirit, went and overthrew the adversary, so must you after holy baptism and the mystical Chrism, clad in the armor of the Holy Spirit, stand firm against the forces of the Enemy and overthrow them, saying: "I can do all things in the Christ who strengthens me."[6]

On the occasion of his baptism in the Jordan, Jesus is officially designated Messiah, and in his humanity he receives in an evident way a more abundant gift of the Holy Spirit.

Immediately, he is led out into the desert, where he will face the temptations of the devil. They are the first signs of the struggle he will sustain against the powers of darkness, over which he will triumph by dying and rising again. Let us note that an open battle begins, even in Jesus' life, after that abundant gift of the Holy Spirit, which has been compared to our confirmation, which, we have said, arms us for battle. Furthermore, after these events, Jesus begins his public life, his activity for the benefit of the society he lives in: He preaches and works miracles.

Therefore two things follow the Spirit's anointing: struggle and social action. The confirmed person acquires two new capabilities: greater strength in the struggle against evil and the ability to engage in action in the midst of the church.

These same effects are discovered in what can be called the first confirmation in the history of the world: Pentecost. On the occasion of Pentecost, Peter cites the text of Joel in his preaching: "I will pour out my Spirit on all flesh" (2:17ff.). That Spirit whom the Father lavished on his Son in the Jordan becomes, after Jesus' death and resurrection, a gift accessible to every creature. The Holy Spirit is dynamism, it is diffusive power, and it is not meant to vivify only the humanity of Christ but, beginning with him, is intended to vivify and transform every creature.

On the occasion of Pentecost, we see the same effects reproduced in the apostles that the gift of the Holy Spirit had worked on Jesus. The apostles, until then fearful and timid, acquire strength to withstand difficulties and persecutions, even confronting the greatest dangers with peace. At the same time, they begin to preach and baptize, that is, to undertake social action in the newborn church.

So we can say that the effects of the anointing of the Holy Spirit on Jesus in the Jordan are the same as those that the Holy Spirit exercises on the apostles at Pentecost and on every Christian at confirmation. The likeness to Christ, initial at baptism and perfected at confirmation, is nonetheless intended to grow and constantly become more perfect, given the immeasurable height of the model whom we must resemble. Confirmation really perfects our garment of worship, which we will need to participate in the eucharistic banquet. Like baptism, confirmation reaches out to the eucharist and only finds its full meaning in it, which is the center and purpose of the whole series of sacraments. The eucharist has been compared by the Fathers to the miracle that Elijah worked in the widow of Zarephath's son (1 Kings 17:8ff.): The prophet brings the boy back to life by stretching out on top of him, that is, by means of direct contact of his own body with the boy's. In this way the eucharist, by establishing *communion* among us and the risen Christ, brings us gradually back to life, always engraving his likeness more deeply on us.

THE BLESSING OF THE CHRISM

The chrism is blessed by the bishop on Holy Thursday morning during the Chrism Mass, with the following words:

> Let us pray
> that God our almighty Father
> will bless this oil
> so that all who are anointed with it
> may be inwardly transformed
> and come to share in eternal salvation.

At this point the bishop breathes over the opening of the vessel of chrism and continues:

> God our maker,
> source of all growth in holiness,
> accept the joyful thanks and praise
> we offer in the name of your church.
> In the beginning, at your command,
> the earth produced fruit-bearing trees.
> From the fruit of the olive tree
> you have provided us with oil for holy chrism.
> The prophet David sang of the life and joy
> that the oil would bring us in the sacraments of your love.

After the avenging flood,
the dove returning to Noah with an olive branch
announced your gift of peace.
This was a sign of a greater gift to come.
Now the waters of baptism wash away the sins of men,
and by the anointing with olive oil
you make us radiant with your joy.

At your command,
Aaron was washed with water,
and your servant Moses, his brother,
anointed him priest.
This too foreshadowed greater things to come.
After your Son, Jesus Christ our Lord,
asked John for baptism in the waters of Jordan,
you sent the Spirit upon him
in the form of a dove
and by the witness of your own voice
you declared him to be your only, well-beloved Son.
In this you clearly fulfilled the prophecy of David,
that Christ would be anointed with the oil of gladness
beyond his fellow men.

(All the concelebrants extended their right hands toward the
chrism, without saying anything, until the end of the prayer.)

And so, Father, we ask you to bless + this oil you have created.
Fill it with the power of the your Holy Spirit
through Christ your Son.
It is from him that chrism takes its name
and with chrism you have anointed
for yourself priests and kings,
prophets and martyrs.

Make this chrism a sign of life and salvation
for those who are to be born again in the waters of baptism.
Wash away the evil they have inherited from sinful Adam,
and when they are anointed with this holy oil

make them temples of your glory,
radiant with the goodness of life
that has its source in you.

Through this sign of chrism
grant them royal, priestly and prophetic honor,
and clothe them with incorruption.
Let this be indeed the chrism of salvation
for those who will be born again of water and the Holy Spirit.
May they come to share eternal life
in the glory of your kingdom.
We ask this through Christ our Lord. Amen.

The blessing of the chrism begins with a kind of *sacred history* of the oil: Even at the beginning of the world, God, in creating olive trees, had in mind the sanctification of humanity. During the Old Covenant established by God with Noah, oil is the sign of a renewed harmony and therefore a new bond between God and humanity. In the Jewish covenant, oil is the sign and tool of the priestly consecration of Aaron. In some way, David presaged the special function of the oil. Finally, in the baptism of Jesus in the Jordan, the Spirit sent by the Father seals the new bond between Jesus and the Father, a bond that is destined to spread in every Christian by means of confirmation.

Thus it seems that confirmation is present in the cosmic plan of God, and we can consider that moment of our sacramental life as the point of arrival of thousands of years' history which the sacrament concentrates in itself and renews. The blessing of the chrism points out various aspects of our likeness to Christ by specifying the powers conferred by the sacrament. Oil was used to consecrate priests, kings, prophets and martyrs. With chrism, the Christian in some way becomes priest, king, prophet and martyr. Confirmation reaches out to the eucharist; it confers a particular priestly character on the one who receives it because it enables that person in a particular way to receive the Father's gift and to offer to God one's whole self in response.

The royal dignity relates to the capability conferred on the Christian by confirmation to provide not only for oneself but also for others, and thus for working in God's kingdom. Moreover, the person anointed with chrism can be called "prophet" as one who preaches and confesses Christ, not necessarily with words but with one's life. The balsam that together with oil makes up the chrism is a perfume. This makes explicit that those who have been anointed with chrism are called to be the "good fragrance of Christ": Christians' actions must make one think of the invisible presence of Christ in them.

Finally, the priestly, royal and prophetic dignity acquired at confirmation commits the Christian completely, even to the point of martyrdom. The threefold dignity acquired in confirmation clarifies the reality of the likeness to Christ: Christ who is the unique and eternal priest, king of a kingdom that is not of this world, more than a prophet since he is the very Word of God, greater than any martyr.

LITURGICAL HISTORY OF CONFIRMATION

The name of this sacrament, which has undergone gradual change throughout the centuries, helps us to understand its meaning and the development of its external form. In the Acts of the Apostles (8:17), confirmation is designated as the "imposition of the hands." Only from the fourth century does it take on the name "confirmation" contemporaneously with the development of the doctrine that considers confirmation the sacrament of virility and perfection of the Christian life. Toward the fifth century in the West, the terms *signaculum* (signing) and *consignatio* (sealing), already used in baptism, are also used for confirmation, where the sign of the cross made on the forehead becomes obviously important. So it seems — as we will see later — that a change occurred in the focal point of the sacrament: The attention that first focused on the imposition of the hands now switches to the sign of the cross, which indicates more clearly the total and definitive consecration to Christ.

The other name for confirmation — *chrismation* — comes from chrism (i.e. oil, unction) and indicates the gesture of anointing and the material, or matter, of the sacrament. The Greeks are accustomed to speaking of *myron,* a perfumed oil, with reference to the "good fragrance of Christ" that the Christian must spread.

THE IMPOSITION OF THE HANDS

In the Acts of the Apostles (8:15 – 17, 19) it is clearly pointed out that confirmation was performed through the imposition of the hands *(cheirotonia).* The gesture was naturally accompanied by a prayer that declared its purpose and meaning: They "prayed for them that they might receive the Holy Spirit." This is an epiclesis, that is, an invocation of the Holy Spirit.

In the most ancient tradition of the African church there was, in addition to these two elements of the imposition of the hands and the epiclesis, the *consignatio,* that is, the tracing of the sign of the cross. It does not appear, however, that this was done with oil. St. Cyprian says: "Among us, we have the custom that those who have been baptized are brought to the bishops in the church and by means of our prayer [invocation to the Holy Spirit] and the imposition of the hands, they receive the Holy Spirit and are completed with the sign of the Lord." It is nonetheless the imposition of the hands that occupies the most important place in the rite.

In order to understand the meaning of the gestures that accompany the conferring of the sacraments, we need to remember that the sacraments are acts of Christ. Now we will look again for the meaning of these gestures, first in the gospels to see if Jesus himself used them, and then at their use as reported in the Old Testament and possibly in Judaism, since it is from that world that Jesus took them. Although Jesus gives a new content to the Old Testament and Judaic usages and customs, these gestures must still preserve something of the world they come from. And recognizing them in their context is certainly illuminating for our purposes as well.

In the gospels, Jesus blesses and heals through the imposition of hands. The healings Jesus performs by means of the imposition of hands are quite numerous; he also used to bless children by laying his hands on them. The gesture must have consisted of resting one or both hands on the head of the person being blessed, establishing a physical contact between the person who blesses and the one blessed, as is still done in the ordination of a priest. Thus the gesture was truly a *sign* of the transmission of a particular power from the person who blesses to the person who is the object of the blessing. In the Old Testament, and still in Jewish liturgy, the imposition of hands accompanies the priestly blessing that Aaron and his descendants can give, and it is accompanied by the solemn formula: "The Lord bless you and keep you; the Lord make his face to shine upon you, and be gracious to you; the Lord lift up his countenance upon you, and give you peace" (Numbers 6:24–26).

Quite special is the imposition of hands on the Levites by the representatives of the people (Numbers 8:10). The Levites made up the tribe the Lord had taken "to serve in the Temple," standing in some way for the people who were all a priestly people but who, practically speaking, could not all perform the religious service in the Temple. Through their representatives, the people laid their hands on the Levites to indicate that they identified with them and that through them they carried out the priestly function that it was their duty and right to do. Through the imposition of hands, a sort of transferral of everyone's priestly power took place upon those who actually performed the worship.

On occasions that included sacrifices, the person offering them would lay his hands on the thing being offered in order to put himself in its situation. The thing being offered somehow became the offering person himself, inasmuch as he transferred his personality to it. On the Day of Atonement (Leviticus 16), the priest would lay his hands on the head of the goat that was to be sent into the wilderness, confessing at the same time his own and the people's sins, that is, transferring to the animal the wrongs for which he and the people were responsible. It can be concluded from this that the imposition of hands always indicates the handing on of something from one person to another: It could be the handing on of power (healing), of interior riches (in the blessing) or interior poverty (in the case of the goat), or even of one's own person.

It is in the Western Church that the custom of accompanying the imposition of the hands with the anointing of the head *(chrismation)* was born. In the tradition of Hippolytus we read:

> Then pouring the consecrated oil from the hand and placing it on the head, say: I anoint you with the holy oil in God the Father Almighty and in Christ Jesus and in the Holy Spirit. And making the sign of the cross on the forehead, kiss the person and say: The Lord be with you, and let the person who received the sign of the cross say: And with your Spirit. Let it be done thus to each one.[7]

THE ANOINTING

The custom of anointing with chrism (done with the sign of the cross), together with the imposition of hands, spread from the Carolingian period (ninth century) on. The imposition of hands, which at the beginning had first place as it appears from the Acts of the Apostles, relinquished its position to the anointing with oil. The current rite directs that the bishop anoints in the form of the cross, with his right hand placed on the head of the person being confirmed. It seems, therefore, that a change occurred in the material of the sacrament. Jesus always spoke in a general way of the gift of the Holy Spirit, tying it neither to specific acts nor to specific words; both were prescribed by the church, and therefore we understand how they could have changed over the course of centuries.

The origin of anointing will also be found in Jewish liturgy. In the Old Testament, people were anointed (Aaron was anointed as high priest, and priests in general were anointed) and so were sacred things (the altar, the ark, the tabernacle of the covenant). Kings too were anointed, and in this context the person anointed *par excellence* is the Messiah.

Everything — people and things — that enjoys a particular relationship with God and has a specific function to perform is anointed. The consecrated oil is in fact a vehicle of a particular power whose source is God, a power that enriches the recipient by binding that person in a special way to God and the world of God. In other words, the oil consecrates. Through the anointing, the Spirit of God descends on the one anointed and transforms the person radically. After he had anointed King Saul, Samuel said to him: "Then the spirit of the Lord will possess you . . . and you will be turned into a different person" (1 Samuel 10:6ff). Again speaking of Saul, we read: "God gave him another heart." And we know that in the Bible, "heart" indicates the person as a whole.

The transformation effected by the anointing empowers the recipient for particular functions. The church anoints those who are being baptized and confirmed as well as those who are being consecrated as priests. Among objects, the church anoints altars. If we consider the anointing of confirmation in light of what has been said, we will see that it confers new riches on the recipient that transform one into a different person, one who has become a more complete image of Christ. Moreover, confirmation empowers the person for particular functions by helping the anointed to radiate the riches that have been received from God.

---

1. Le Christ, (Paris, 1954), 242 – 243.

2. M. Miletti, *Storia Liturgica,* vol. IV (Milano), 83.

3. It is now the practice of the Latin church that priests who baptize a person who has reached the age of reason are, by virtue of the law, to confirm that person at the same time.

4. *Baptismal Catechesis* XVII, 14. From *The Works of Saint Cyril of Jerusalem,* vol. 2, in *The Fathers of the Church,* vol. 64 (Washington: The Catholic University of America Press, 1970), 105.

5. *Mystagogical Catechesis* III. From *The Works of Saint Cyril of Jerusalem,* 168-169.

6. Ibid., 4.

7. Righetti, *Storia Liturgica,* vol. 3 (Milano: 1956), 153 –154.

The Eucharist

FOR AS OFTEN AS YOU

EAT THIS BREAD AND DRINK THE CUP,

YOU PROCLAIM THE LORD'S DEATH

UNTIL HE COMES.

1 CORINTHIANS 11:26

The Jewish Passover Banquet

THOSE WHO HAVE RECEIVED BAPTISM AND CONFIR-
mation complete their Christian initiation in the eucharist. Their
incorporation into Christ reaches in the eucharist that level
where by participating in it, they will progress and grow each
and every day.

The life of Jesus reaches its culmination in the Last
Supper, death and resurrection by fulfilling the redemptive plan
of the Father. Jesus' entire life was a continuous gift of himself
to the Father and to humanity. However, in the Last Supper and
in his death and resurrection, this gift was made explicit and
concrete in the most complete way. These are the events that the
church celebrates in the Paschal Triduum, from Thursday
evening through the Easter Vigil, which takes place between
Saturday night and Sunday morning. Calling the three days by
one name highlights the fact that the events that took place
during this time were not independent events; they made up
one great event that began in the cenacle, or upper room.

What happened in the cenacle on Thursday night? In
order to answer this question, it is necessary to place the
liturgical act Jesus performs on that occasion in its context. The
context is the Jewish Passover banquet (the *seder*, which means
ordo, an order of worship), that is, the domestic liturgy that
every Jewish person used to celebrate (and still celebrates today)
as a memorial of the liberation from Egypt.

The majority of scholars agree that at the Last Supper,
Jesus celebrated the Jewish passover rite with his apostles but
added a new element to it. This is not clearly stated in the
gospels; indeed, the Fathers of the church argue whether Jesus
celebrated a real and proper paschal banquet in the cenacle or a

simple meal that was religious in nature. This is not clear in the gospels. Actually, according to the synoptic gospels, it seems that Jesus celebrated the banquet on the first day of unleavened bread, whereas according to John (18:39), it appears that the crucifixion took place on the first day of unleavened bread, thus on the same day and more or less at the same hour when the lambs that would be eaten during the paschal banquet were sacrificed in the Temple. The discussions on this subject are far from exhausted.

The scarcity of details in the gospel accounts pertaining to this question could be proof that it really was a paschal banquet. These accounts tell us only the new things that happened on that occasion, skipping over all the other details because they were reporting a ritual banquet that was celebrated every year; the authors considered it superfluous to describe it in full detail.

However things actually unfolded, it is certain that the Last Supper takes place against a paschal background, which means renewal, waiting and hope. This event took place in the month of *Nisan* (March – April), the month when, according to the most current Jewish tradition, the world was created. It is the month of astronomical spring and of the springtime of the world. Jewish thought, however, never turns to the past in a nostalgic attitude. If it does look back in time, it does so only to animate hope, which impels us to look toward the future. Indeed, it is in the month of *Nisan,* when nature renews itself, that the Messiah will come, bringing to all persons and things the renewal about which the prophets spoke. Between these two points of history, the beginning and the completion, the Jew celebrates the Passover, the memorial of the liberation from Egypt.

According to some texts dated a bit later than Jesus' lifetime, the Passover banquet was held at the beginning of the Christian era substantially the way it is now, with the exception of some not very important additions made over the centuries. Here, briefly, is the outline of the celebration according to the current ritual, from which we will be able to retrace the order of the celebration performed by Jesus.

After the blessing of the day for the feast of Passover, said over the first cup of wine, all the special foods required for the occasion, including, of course, the unleavened bread *(masah)*, are brought before the leader of the banquet. Three unleavened breads are brought. Then the head of the banquet breaks one, covering a part of it with a napkin and putting the other part with the unbroken breads. When the second cup of wine is filled, which will be drunk later, everything is ready for the narration *(haggadah)* of the history of Israel, which we would call the liturgy of the word.

The narration unfolds by means of questions addressed to the leader of the banquet concerning the special character of the night of the Passover, during which, as opposed to other nights, only unleavened bread, bitter herbs (and no others) and roasted rather than boiled meat are eaten. This questioning gives the cue to the father of the family to explain the meaning of the feast, and he must do so, the Mishnah says, "by beginning with the disgrace and ending with the exaltation."

The leader of the banquet first gives a brief response, remembering that "we were slaves of Pharaoh in Egypt, and God brought our people out with a strong hand and a promise of redemption." The narration is then taken up again in detailed form by reading and scrutinizing scripture in depth, especially Deuteronomy (26:5ff.) and Joshua (24:2ff.). These are the two oldest accounts of the history of the salvation of Israel that take into consideration its two principal events: the calling of the patriarchs, who were taken from a pagan land by the Lord so that they could take possession of the land promised to the people of God, and the liberation from slavery to the Egyptians. The liberation is an event of fundamental importance in Israel's history because this is when the promise made to Abraham was fulfilled with the final possession of the land, the birth of the real and truly free people, and, above all, the establishment through the Torah of a new bond between Israel and its God.

Memorial and Thanksgiving

IN THIS CELEBRATION WE HAVE AN EXAMPLE OF *memorial.* Here one lingers in recalling past history, not to look back nostalgically but to be aware that what the Lord has done for Israel is always a present reality. The celebration is the means offered to every Jew to "consider oneself as having been led out of Egypt." It is the means by which every Jew can continue to live in that current of liberation and salvation that has its source in the Exodus from Egypt and that the ritual elements aim to reconstruct. Nonetheless, the ritual does not stop at the present moment in time but, in the spirit of invocation and desire, turns to the moment when the Messiah will come. Thus the Jewish Passover *seder* is articulated in three fundamental moments in time, all of which are lived in a concentrated form in the celebration. The leader of the banquet explains the reason for the custom of eating roast lamb, unleavened bread and bitter herbs by linking them to the events of the Exodus: The Passover ritual in which special foods play a part is the way in which each Jew relives and actualizes past history.

The Passover lamb *(pesah)* recalls how the Lord "passed over" (in Hebrew *pasah*) the houses of the Israelites at the moment of the death of the Egyptians' firstborn sons. Unleavened bread refers to the fact that during the act of being led out of Egypt, there was no time to let bread rise. The bitter herbs recall the bitterness suffered during slavery. Yet that previous history is never completely past, since it is reactualized in every Jew who celebrates the rite of Passover, in every Jew who must "consider oneself as having been led out of Egypt" again, according to the Mishnah. The liberation the Lord worked at the time of Moses is the liberation of every individual Israelite, and the rite is the means of becoming conscious of that and participating in it. After this, the praying of the first part of the Psalms of Praise begins (called in Hebrew *hallel*), that is, Psalms 113 and 114.

The second cup of wine, which was prepared before the narration began, is taken at this point. Then, taking the piece of unleavened bread that was broken, two blessings are said over it. The first blessing is the customary blessing for bread: "Blessed are you, Lord our God, Ruler of the universe, who brings forth bread from the earth." A special blessing is then said: "Blessed are you, Lord our God, Ruler of the universe, who sanctified us with your commandments and commanded us to eat the unleavened bread." At this point, the unleavened bread is distributed to those at the table.

This first part of the celebration concludes now with the meal. The "blessing of the food" (what we would call "thanksgiving") follows. There is a recitation over a third cup of wine, accompanied by prayers that have an especially messianic content: They ask for the reconstruction of Jerusalem, the coming of David "your messiah." "Let Elijah the prophet and the Messiah, son of David, your servant, come in our time and bring us the good news."

The thanksgiving concludes with the blessing of another cup of wine, the fourth. The blessing of this fourth cup of wine is very solemn. It is the cup that the Jews used to say only David was worthy to bless, thus clearly ascribing a messianic character to it. This is accompanied by the recitation of other psalms of praise, beginning with Psalm 115 ("Not to us, O LORD, not to us, but to your name give glory") and ending with Psalm 118. Verse 26 of Psalm 118 is to be particularly stressed by having all participants recite it in chorus: "Blessed is the one who comes in the name of the LORD."

This invocation is the welcome to the Messiah, who can be expected at any moment. Thus everything concludes with praise to God, who redeems his people.

The Last Supper

WHAT HAPPENED ON THAT THURSDAY EVENING AT the cenacle? Let's see what other New Testament sources tell us. In First Corinthians 11:23 – 26, dated AD 54 – 56, Paul stresses that he "hands on" what he has "received"; therefore a "tradition" concerning the account of the Last Supper has already developed. In fact, the form of this passage reflects a liturgy that is already consolidated and structured (see, for example, the double repetition: "Do this in remembrance of me"). Therefore, it depends on a narrative that predates it.

Of the evangelists, only John concentrates on the washing of the feet, which is introduced with great solemnity (13:1ff). The account of the institution of the eucharist is found in the three synoptics. In these we can distinguish "two formulations independent of each other from the same tradition,"[1] one of which belongs to Mark, to which Matthew referred. Mark's passage does not seem to fit well into this gospel. One might think that the evangelist had found an already existing text relating to the Last Supper and that it must have been already so authoritative that he would not change it to make it uniform within his context; instead, he inserted it as it was. Linguistic investigation shows a strong Semitic character that constitutes a guarantee of antiquity, since the original account was certainly in Hebrew or Aramaic. Dates given by recent and authoritative studies for Mark's text vary between AD 40 and 50. "This tradition, then, falls in the first decade"[2] after the event took place.

The other formulation is Paul's, to which Luke referred; in these two texts one can note a certain Hellenistic character in the use of terms with respect to Mark. At any rate, in both formulations we go back to a date fairly close to the event.

At this point, we would like to pose the question of whether it is possible to identify at what moment in the domestic Jewish Passover rite Jesus inserted his words, those words that no one in the world had ever heard before: "Take this and eat it;

this is my body," and "Take this and drink from it; this is my blood," those words that offered a response to the prayer for the coming of the messianic redemption: Today it is fulfilled. In regard to the reconstruction of the domestic Passover rite celebrated by Jesus, various attempts have been made to answer this question, and what we have said here is obviously only conjecture.

From the sparse information the gospels provide, we know that "during the meal" Jesus washes the apostles' feet (John 13:1), that he consecrates the bread at a time different from when the wine is consecrated after the meal (Luke 22:20), and that before leaving the cenacle he sings some hymns (Mark 14:26; Matthew 26:30). Each of those actions mentioned by the evangelists are verified in corresponding actions customary to the Passover banquet, actions that, at the Last Supper, acquired a new aspect. It seems that we can pinpoint the moment of the washing of the feet: when a basin is brought to the leader of the banquet at the beginning of the meal so that he might wash his hands before reciting the blessing of the bread. Jesus makes a particular use of that washing, but its newness is grafted onto a customary action in the ritual.

And so we ask if Jesus' words over the bread — those words that break the confines of any traditional ritual — were not said after the formula we quoted above and which every Jew still recites today, namely, the breaking of the bread: "Blessed are you, Lord our God, who brings forth bread from the earth." These words — in the context of the Last Supper, when death was impending and the apostles, although unaware, must have felt it weighing on them — almost seem to assume the tone and value of a prophecy of the resurrection. The identification between the bread and the Body of Christ was explicit in Jesus' words (and this fact will be particularly highlighted by Paul), so one may assume that just as the Lord brings forth bread from the earth so would the Lord draw forth that body from the earth.

The New Covenant

BASED ON THE PARTICULARS OF THE PASSOVER MEAL, we ask ourselves if it is not possible to identify the piece of unleavened bread which is blessed twice and thus already imbued with an especially sacred character, as was the unleavened bread which Jesus consecrated and gave to his apostles to eat.

There are a variety of conjectures about this; what we have proposed is but one among many. Given that Luke says expressly that the wine is consecrated *after* the meal, it seems possible to identify the cup Jesus consecrates as that cup which every Jew used to bless and still blesses with special solemnity at the closing of every Passover meal.

We said that Jewish tradition attributes a particular messianic character to that cup of wine and that it is David himself who is awaited — that is, the prototype of the Messiah — to come and bless it. The Psalms of Praise accompanying the blessing seem especially fitting to that experience that the table companions of the Last Supper were living; even more, it seems that several psalms, such as Psalm 116, cannot be explained except in that context. In Psalm 116 the anguish of death alternates with the assurance of the Lord's help, in a faith we can define as faith in the resurrection.

The Last Supper ends with the singing of hymns, which the evangelists speak of and we can recognize as the Psalms of Praise that close the Passover banquet. The Passover rite, which is both new and old at the same time, is now concluded. On this evening the apostles could have applied that invocation which expresses the greatest desire of all Jews — "Blessed is he who comes in the name of the Lord!" — to a person who had been clearly identified.

Once again, Jesus inserts the new deed he performs into the framework of Jewish liturgy. Just as at Nazareth, when Jesus wanted the synagogue worship to form the background against which to announce that the salvation proclaimed by the prophets was now present in his person, so too the essential moment of his earthly life, that moment when Jesus celebrates his sacrifice in liturgical form, is inserted in the framework of Jewish worship, worship that he lives, takes to himself and brings forward.

That history of salvation which the leader of the banquet recapitulates for his table companions by citing the beginning and the determining moment of the Exodus, that salvation history whose conclusion is envisioned by the prophets' preaching in the context of the messianic era, that history, without losing its eschatological tension, now has reached a point of particular fullness. The presence of the "bridegroom" in the upper room in Jerusalem represents a new relationship with God ("the cup of the new covenant") without, however, making the invocation to the Messiah superfluous, namely, that the Messiah "come soon, in our days." He is present in the world, and yet the Book of Revelation concludes with the invocation: "Maranatha! Come, Lord Jesus!" The refrain "Blessed is he who comes in the name of the Lord" is applied to Jesus in the cenacle and in Christian liturgy without, however, ceasing the invocation that Christ come soon to complete the work entrusted to him by the Father.

That evening in the "upper room" of a house in Jerusalem, a new period in salvation history was initiated, a point of fruition and at the same time a point of departure, turned to the awaiting of the final fulfillment, toward the return in glory of Christ, the parousia, when "God will be all in all." Both the Passover banquet and the Last Supper are turned and projected toward the future, with a single difference: In the former, there is the waiting for a day that will come, what the prophets call "that day," whereas at the Last Supper, "that day" (a technical expression the prophets use to refer to the messianic time) has already begun. In other words, there is a diversity in perspective. The Jewish Passover, as well as the Last Supper, are oriented toward the future; but what is awaited in the Passover ritual has yet to begin, whereas in the Last Supper it has already begun and is waiting to be completed.

The Eucharist in the Easter Triduum

THE EASTER MYSTERY CONSISTS IN THE DEATH AND resurrection of Christ. We celebrate the Easter mystery every day in the eucharist, yet Sunday has "a preeminence in the week." In the liturgical year, it is Easter that has preeminence (*General Norms for the Liturgical Year and Calendar,* 8).

Easter is celebrated over three days called the Easter Triduum, which begins on Holy Thursday evening with the Mass of the Lord's Supper. The celebrations of Friday and the Vigil between Saturday night and Sunday morning reveal the Easter mystery primarily in its historical dimension, whereas the Holy Thursday celebration communicates and makes this mystery live in its natural dimension.[3] In order to probe more deeply into the meaning and scope of the Easter mystery, let us try to see and understand what happened on the first "Holy Thursday" in that upper room in Jerusalem in the light of the events that took place later that evening and on the following days.

On Friday, the drama reaches its culmination with the death of Jesus, preceded by horrible acts of violence preserved for us in the gospel accounts. Jesus' attitude of self-offering, which characterizes his whole life, now finds its visible and cruel epilogue on Calvary.

The Last Supper takes place around a table in the context of a liturgically oriented banquet which is, however, festive. The link between the two moments is found in the new words that Jesus inserts into the ritual of the Passover banquet: "Take this and eat it" and "Take this and drink from it." We must see in these words the interpretation of what will happen the next day. Calvary will add the visible dimension of the action of self-offering that had been already completed in Jesus. Jesus did not want the culminating moment of his life to come about only in the brutal act of bloodshed; rather he wanted to place this act of self-offering in the context of a liturgical action.

With his words at the Last Supper, Jesus wanted to explain to us the significance of Good Friday in particular as

well as of the entire paschal event. What would we have understood of the significance of Good Friday if Jesus had not given
us the interpretation? Although the interpretation does not take
the tragedy away from the drama, by putting it in the context
of liturgy it does endow it with the grandeur and the dignity of
a celebration.

With his words at the Last Supper, Jesus makes us
understand that the offering of himself "for many" is an offering
that, before the brutality of the external act took place, has been
fulfilled in the secrecy of love. We can consider that Jesus places
his life in such a higher realm — the hands of the Father —
that in reality "no one takes it from me," as he says in John 10:18.
In order to grasp the import of this paschal event, we must
view it in the context of the extremely close union that links
Thursday, Friday and the dawn of Sunday. In the ritual of
the Passover banquet, we have already seen that there are several
words that can be interpreted as expressions of faith in the
resurrection. Jesus' own words over the bread that is "his body"
are closely connected to the "Blessed are you, Lord our God, King
of the world, who brings forth bread from the earth." Psalm
118:17 explicitly says: "I shall not die, but I shall live, and recount
the deeds of the LORD."

The offering Jesus makes of himself must be viewed
against the background of the entire biblical tradition that dates
back to the sacrifice of Isaac, in which the Christian tradition
sees the expression of faith in the resurrection. On Thursday
evening, Jesus initiates his own followers into the entirety
of the paschal mystery by celebrating it together with them in
anticipation of his death and resurrection. Jesus continues to do
so throughout time by actualizing the paschal mystery in the
eucharistic celebration. Therefore, there is a direct connection
between the table on that first Holy Thursday and our eucharistic table. However, the similarity in their form must not make
us forget that the paschal mystery is already celebrated in its
entirety at the Last Supper, and at our eucharistic table it is the
Christ who conquered death who is present.

The Eucharist in the History of Salvation

EVERY EUCHARIST, INASMUCH AS IT IS A MEMORIAL, presents itself as an event of history by actualizing the past events and by extending them toward fulfillment and in some way anticipating it. Nonetheless, while this fullness in Christ is already complete, it is not yet complete in us Christians. Every eucharist, then, is positioned as a present reality, in balance between the past and the future (see Part 1, Liturgy in the Biblical Tradition: The Memorial, page 11).

Now we will see in greater detail how this reality is expressed in our liturgy. The fourth eucharistic prayer of the Roman Missal begins with praise of the Father Creator. Then, although very quickly, it touches upon the principal stages in the history of salvation: original sin and God's faithful love for sinful humanity; the covenant God offers to Abraham and then to Moses; and the calling of the prophets. Then it centers briefly on the incarnation of Jesus, his preaching and his sacrifice by which "he has destroyed death and restored life."

All this would be merely past history if we did not make a memorial of it in the celebration, that is, if Jesus had not left us the mystery we celebrate as "eternal covenant," open to the participation of all generations. In this way, history becomes present because I, today, can take part in it: "Every Christian must consider oneself as present at the Easter event."

The tending toward the third moment in history is already expressed in the proclamation of the mystery of faith, "until you come in glory," and is taken up again and made explicit in the words that follow: "Looking forward to his coming in glory, we offer. . . ." The final Amen is the anticipation, as yet still partial, of the hymn in chorus with which the whole of redeemed humanity, together with every creature, will render "honor and glory" to God forever.

Throughout its whole liturgical tradition, the church has always lived its eucharistic memorial in this way. I will give two examples of ancient anaphorae (liturgical prayers). The first anaphora is by St. Hippolytus, a third-century doctor of the church. It begins like this:

> We give You thanks, O God,
> through your beloved Child Jesus Christ,
> whom you have sent us in the last days
> as Savior, Redeemer, and Messenger of your will.
> He is your Word, inseparable from you,
> through whom you have created everything
> and in whom you find your delight.
>
> You sent him from heaven
> into the womb of a Virgin.
> He was conceived and became flesh.
> He manifested himself as your Son
> born of the Spirit and the Virgin.
> He did your will,
> and, to win for you a holy people,
> he stretched out his hands in suffering
> to rescue from suffering
> those who believe in you.

Here, the first two points of the outline are obvious: the creation, the incarnation and the passion. The anaphora continues:

> When he was about to surrender himself to voluntary suffering
> in order to destroy death,
> to break the devil's chains,
> to tread hell underfoot,
> to pour out his light upon the just,
> to establish the covenant
> and manifest his resurrection,
> he took bread,
> he gave you thanks and said:
> "Take, eat, this is my body
> which is broken for you."
> In like manner for the cup, he said:
> "This is my blood
> which is poured out for you."[4]

Having noted the creation, incarnation and passion, it continues with the account of the institution of the eucharist, with Jesus' command: "Do this in memory [as a memorial] of me." Thus we reach the present moment of time in the celebration. The third moment in time is not made explicit, but it is therein that the "all glory and honor" which is given to the Father anticipates the eschatological praise. The anaphora we have cited is from the Roman tradition. The style is spare and typically Latin.

I will give another example of an anaphora belonging to the Eastern tradition: It is from Book VIII of the *Apostolic Constitution,* a ritual text of rites that is held to be Hebraic in origin and adapted to the needs of Christian worship. Here the history of salvation is narrated with many details and also concludes with the institution of the eucharist. I will cite a few passages:

It is truly right and just to praise you first of all, the only true God. . . . You called things from nothingness into existence through your only begotten Son. . . .

Through him, O eternal God, you created everything, and through him you take care of all things in accordance with your prevenient providence. Through him you have bestowed the gift of being, and through him you have bestowed the gift of existing in the good. God and Father of your only-begotten Son, through him you created, in the first place, the Cherubim and Seraphim. . . .

Through him you then create the visible world and all it contains. You stretch out the heavens like a vault, you unfold it like a tent. . . .

You create the day and the night. You bring the light forth from your treasury, and when it withdraws, you send the darkness so that the living things that move upon the earth may have their rest. You establish the sun in the firmament to rule over the day, and the moon to rule over the night, with the choir of stars in heaven to sing of your magnificence.

You created the water to slake thirst and cleanse, the life-giving air for breathing and speaking. . . .

You created the fire to comfort us in the darkness, to help us in our needs, to warm us and give us light.

Then follows the creation of man and woman. The account of the Fall is particularly prominent. The flood is mentioned, as are all the various benefits lavished on the chosen people, among which the liberation from Egypt is especially emphasized. At this point the "Sanctus" is brought in, which marks an interruption in the unfolding development of the history of salvation. Then it continues:

You are holy indeed, infinitely holy, the Most High exalted for ever. Holy too is your only-begotten Son, our Lord and God, Jesus Christ! In all things he served you, his God and Father, who are admirable in your creation and worthy of being celebrated for your providence. He did not scorn the human race that was being lost. . . .

Then the text brings in many details of the birth of Jesus (from which lineage and city) and the account of his life and the miracles he performed. Then it goes on to describe the passion in great detail, and this marks the central point, which is followed by the institution of the eucharist. The text then concludes:

Mindful then of his passion, of his death,
of his resurrection from the dead,
of his return to heaven, of his second coming in the future
when he will come with glory and power
to judge the living and the dead
and render to each according to his works,
we offer you, O King and God,
according to your testament, this bread and cup.[5]

The waiting for the second coming of Jesus is explicit here and forms one of the essential points of the prayer. Therefore it can be said that the Christian people through its entire tradition has lived the eucharistic moment in its threefold dimensions in time.

The Holy Spirit in the Eucharist

ALREADY IN THE OLDEST LITURGICAL TRADITION OF the church we find two constant elements in the eucharistic prayer: an invocation to God, asking the Father to send the Holy Spirit to sanctify the gifts being offered (epiclesis), and an account of the Supper, that is, the words with which Christ expressed his will that the bread and wine become the signs of his presence.

These two elements are already present in the anaphora of Hippolytus (third century). The idea of the Spirit's cooperation in the consecratory effect of Christ's words is likewise explicit in the East.[6] The respective value of these elements with regard to the consecration, that is, the transformation of the bread and wine into the presence of Christ, is a subject of discussion among scholars.[7]

Some Fathers of the church seem to stress the importance of the words of institution but, in the East at least, the epiclesis was considered consecratory and essential. Augustine seems to give particular value to the words of the Supper: "Take away the word, it is bread and wine. Add the word, and it is something else. And what is this other thing? The Body of Christ, the Blood of Christ." Ambrose of Milan felt the same, whereas Cyril of Jerusalem tended to focus on the epiclesis.

Nonetheless, the Fathers generally considered the eucharistic prayer as a prayer that had, in its entirety, consecratory value with two essential moments: the epiclesis and the account of the Supper. That is to say, the Fathers were not looking for a precise moment when the transformation occurred but saw the entire eucharistic prayer as a consecratory prayer in which the epiclesis and the account of the Supper form an indivisible unity.

Concerning the transformative power of the Spirit, an analogy has been noted between the working of the Holy Spirit in transforming the bread and wine into the body and blood of Christ and the Incarnation. Both take place through the power of the Spirit, whom the Father sends to Mary (Luke 1:35), and at the moment the gifts are being offered. A similar approach is found in the Roman Missal, in the prayer over the gifts on the Fourth Sunday of Advent:

> Lord,
> may the power of the Spirit,
> which sanctified Mary, the mother of your Son,
> make holy the gifts we place upon the altar.

Some authors see in the importance given to the epiclesis a corrective to a possibly magical interpretation of the eucharist: Christ's presence in the midst of his people happens because this is what Jesus wanted, and he said so in an explicit way: "This is my body," and "This is my blood." But repeating these words is neither a way of imposing on God nor of forcing God; the church can only implore God to become present in the person of his Christ. This is what the church does in the epicletic prayer, which thus becomes the expression of our dependence on God, of our incapacity that is resolved only in the invocation. God's presence "cannot be induced, it can only be invoked. *Maranatha!* (O, Lord, come!)" The church prays and implores; it does not command.

The epiclesis comprises two parts, the first of which almost always precedes the account of the Supper and the second of which follows it. In the first, the Father is asked to send the Spirit to sanctify "the gifts," the most important gifts being the bread and wine. However, "gifts" has a wider meaning, since the presence of the believers is really authentic presence only if they too are in some way a "gift," that is, with the disposition to offer, to take part in the offering of Christ.

The second part of the epiclesis asks that the transforming and sanctifying work of the Spirit may come through the consecrated species to those who are nourished by the body and blood of Christ, thereby transforming them into the unity of "one body and one spirit." In the third eucharistic prayer, we read: "Grant that we, who are nourished by his body and blood, may be filled with his Holy Spirit, and become one body, one spirit in Christ." The real and personal presence of Christ in the bread and wine reaches out and extends his presence throughout his mystical body, with the aim of building up his Mystical Body in unity.

Our Participation

LIKE ALL LITURGY, THE EUCHARIST IS A MEMORIAL. In the liturgy we live the death and resurrection of Jesus Christ as well as all preceding history reactualized for us. In this way we prepare for the fulfillment of history, the parousia, and we move toward it in hope and invocation. Therefore, every eucharistic celebration is placed in time like a new link in the chain of history that carries history forward. In fact, every eucharist is at the same time both always the same and always new. It is always the same because the event that is reactualized in it is always this: the unique sacrifice of Jesus Christ that is made present for us. However, at the same time it is new, because throughout time there are always different men and women who are participating in it.

The eucharist is always the same because the principal subject of the memorial is always God, whose will for our salvation is made present and concrete and whose will for our salvation continues to be accomplished in "an effective and creative event." The eucharist is always new in that, on the part of the human creature, there needs to be some response to God's action on our behalf. In the second eucharistic prayer of the Roman Missal, the part that immediately follows the account of the Supper says: "In memory of his death and resurrection, we offer you, Father, this life-giving bread, this saving cup. We thank you for counting us worthy to stand in your presence and serve you." Our participation in the event of the eucharist is to enter into and become part of the event being celebrated, that is, to do what Christ does. Rather than remain a spectator at Christ's sacrifice, we are to become, together with him, an active participant in it. The event we participate in during the eucharistic celebration is Christ's offering to the Father and to humanity. In order that we too can take an active part in the event, we are asked to become "an everlasting gift to you" (Eucharistic Prayer III), "a living sacrifice of praise" (Eucharistic Prayer IV) in resemblance of Christ.

We know that Christ's offering was a global offering comprising his entire life and that this must be the model for Christians. But what does that mean? Let us recall the sacrifice of Abraham: Was that a real sacrifice or not? It was, even though the child was not sacrificed. Sacrifice is not only an offering that is realized in action but also a potential offering, an attitude of total surrender, having the "disposition of" offering and therefore possessing a good but as one that is not ours, enjoying it as on loan. Abraham put his son fully at God's disposal.

What are Christians called to put at God's disposal so that our participation in the eucharist will be real? What goods do we have to offer that will constitute the object of our offering? The answer comes from Jesus' own words: "This is my body," and "This is my blood," that is, his whole self. (In his self-offering, Jesus is the one who offers and the one who is offered. Both are the same, one Christ. The first is active, the second passive, but both require willingness and surrender.) These words are followed by "Do this in memory of me" (for my memorial). Generally these words are understood in the ritual sense: Jesus would have instructed the apostles to repeat exactly what he had done on the occasion of the Supper.

Behind this expression, however, are two formulae: "Do this" and "Do it this way." The first introduces instructions and advice and thus concerns the way of living; the second prescribes the repetition of a rite. We can say, then, that these words point to a twofold memorial: one that is ritual in nature and one that is moral. As such, they are not limited to the moment of celebration, essential as that is; rather, they touch upon every aspect of life. They are not merely a liturgical rubric; instead, they are a program of life.

Disciples and Christians throughout time are to repeat in ritual what the Master did so that the act of worship will also be for them a taking part in what Jesus himself is expressing in it: Life, received as a gift, becomes itself a gift. With those words, Jesus reveals himself as a model of life and source of the way of living for those who believe in him. Following Christ's path, the primary matter or material of the Christian's offering must be one's whole life. One's entire life in all its manifestations must be put at the disposal of the Father: activities, affections and others, up to the acceptance of death.

All the rest makes up the secondary material of the sacrifice and can be the material of one's offering only insofar as it is an expression of one's life. Extrinsic goods (material goods, money and so forth) can constitute the material of the sacrifice as well, but only insofar as they are the expression — even if an external one — of the life of the person who offers them. It is unimaginable that they could substitute for the offering of one's own life.

Christians who unite themselves to Christ's sacrifice know that it means uniting themselves to Jesus, who offered his life to the Father and was glorified by the Father. In the eucharist, this *placing ourselves at the disposal* of God makes us like Christ in his passion, and we know that "if we have been united with him in a death like his, we will certainly be united with him in a resurrection like his" (Romans 6:5ff). These words that Paul speaks on the subject of baptism are all the more valid for the eucharist, which continues and perfects our incorporation into Christ, our baptismal union with Christ.

Christ crucified stands on every altar, but in the ancient church Christ was represented clothed in royal garments, crowned and alive. The crucifix on the altar is really the image of the glorified Christ, the Christ who has reached his glory by passing through the crucifixion. This is the image we ought to have present during the Mass: Our participation in Christ's sacrifice is participation in the paschal Christ, the Christ who suffered and through his suffering reached his glorification.

The Sacrament of the Covenant

IN THE ACCOUNT OF THE SUPPER, THE WORDS relating to the chalice indicate it as the cup "of the new and eternal covenant." The eucharist is the powerful moment of the Christian's relationship with God. That relationship, which the Bible calls *covenant,* is a relationship that is composed of every moment in the believer's life. But it is "condensed," so to speak, in a particular way in the liturgy and, most of all, in the celebration of the eucharist.

All liturgy, we have said, makes real that type of *cosmic breathing* through which we receive everything from God and everything returns to God. This is true especially of the eucharist: The ritual makes us see this dynamism between heaven and earth by means of certain gestures.

The epiclesis, as we have already mentioned, is accompanied by the gesture of the imposition of hands *(cheirotonia)* over the bread and wine. The movement of the celebrant's hands, which are lifted high and then lowered, makes the first moment of the covenant explicit, the moment in which we receive from the Father the greatest gift of the Father's love: The Son who assumed our human nature, died and rose again and is now in our midst. The words ask the Father to send the Holy Spirit so that with the Spirit's transforming power the bread and wine may become for us the presence of the risen Christ.

> Let your Spirit come upon these gifts to make them holy,
> so that they may become for us
> the body and blood of our Lord,
> Jesus Christ. (Eucharistic Prayer II)

The second moment of the covenant,[8] the response on the part of the believers, is expressed at various points in the eucharistic prayer. Yet it is also made explicit by a gesture: lifting up the bread and wine. It is a gesture of offering that synthesizes all the eucharistic action in its aspect as a response to God's gifts. The Christian responds to the Father's gift by offering the greatest good: Christ himself. The believer's own personal offering of self, however, also becomes part of Christ's. The mediator of that response is Christ himself:

> Through him, with him, in him,
> in the unity of the Holy Spirit,
> all glory and honor is yours, almighty Father,
> for ever and ever.

This formula, with simple variations, has been present throughout the Western liturgical tradition since the Roman anaphora of Hippolytus (third century). "Through him . . ." is inspired by the Johannine prologue: "All things came into being through him" (John 1:3). Christ's function as mediator is reinforced by "in him," which appears to recall "Abide in me as I abide in you" in the parable of the true vine (John 15:1ff). "All glory and honor" is taken from Revelation 7:12, which describes the universal liturgy at the end of time and thus is meant to express the eschatological tension of the eucharistic celebration. The concluding "Amen" is the assent of faith on the part of the participants in the liturgy and the expression of their effective participation in Christ's action: It is the "yes" of the believer to all that is done and said in the eucharistic prayer.

Justin Martyr (second century) speaks of it: "All the people present joyfully acclaim: 'Amen.'" In Hebrew, "Amen" means "fiat" — so be it. Later Fathers highlighted the very particular importance of this "Amen." In the third century, Dionysius of Alexandria sums up in this way the various stages of the believer's participation in the Mass: "He has listened to the eucharistic prayer, he has answered 'Amen' with the others, he has approached the altar and stretched out his hand to receive the sacred food."

The two gestures pointed out here appear complementary, the first expressing the gift from above and the second expressing the response that rises from earth to heaven. Therefore the vertical dimension of the covenant is expressed. Another gesture makes us *see* the other dimension of the covenant: the horizontal dimension. The covenant God offers to us is offered to the whole of humanity brought together by the one broken bread.

The "sign of peace" was originally the "kiss of peace" and has occupied different places in the celebration according to the era and rite. In the Anglican liturgy, the "sign of peace" concludes the liturgy of the word, thus pointing to the source of communion among the believers in the Word, in the common confession of faith and acknowledgment of sins. The seventh-century use of the gesture is significant. The celebrant would kiss either the altar or the host first and then exchange the sign of peace. This made it clear that Christ is the primary source of peace. In the current Roman ritual, the sign of peace precedes the breaking of the bread. The believers implore the peace and unity of the church and the whole human family; they express love for one another and beg for peace among all people (*General Instruction of the Roman Missal*, 56b). The current place of the gesture makes it less obvious that the source of peace is the broken bread. It seems to emphasize rather the prior necessity of a state of peace with one's sisters and brothers before receiving communion.

These three gestures are obvious *signs* of the reality of the covenant in which the believer lives with God and thus with his or her sisters and brothers. These three gestures are signs of that relationship which has its source and destination in God (alpha and omega), a relationship which encompasses all the people of God.

Sacrament of Unity

THE TITLE OF THIS SECTION SOUNDS LIKE A REPE-tition of the previous one, "The Sacrament of the Covenant." Nonetheless, we believe that a repetition which will allow us to examine this aspect of the eucharist from another point of view will not be superfluous. Indeed, this is the fundamental reality of the eucharist: to be the efficacious sign of that unity which is meant to be accomplished on earth as a likeness and reflection of the unity of God so "that they all may be one. As you, Father, are in me and I am in you, may they also be in us" (John 17:21).

This unifying power of the eucharist is also expressed by the cross, which is in the center of or beside every altar, and in particular by what is called the cosmic cross, since it is surrounded by a circle, or ring, which represents the entire universe. The top reaches to the sky, the bottom penetrates the depths, and the arms touch east and west, thus unifying the unfolding of history as well.

In the Roman rite, the epiclesis over the believer, which we have discussed, is followed by what are called "intercessory prayers," in which are named the universal church, the whole world and even those who have left this world. The epiclesis and intercessory prayers, whose purpose is to bring all together into the unity of the body of Christ, are closely connected. In the first, the same Spirit who transformed the bread and wine into the presence of the risen Christ is asked to transform the church too, gathering it into unity (Eucharistic Prayer II) so that it might become in Christ "one body and one spirit" (Eucharistic Prayer III). In this prayer God is being asked that all who share in the one bread and one cup as they are gathered together in one body by the Holy Spirit might become "a living sacrifice of praise" (Eucharistic Prayer IV).

Therefore, the Father is asked that the sanctifying and transforming power of the Spirit, by radiating outward from the vital nucleus of the presence of the risen Christ, might also be operative within the community gathered around the altar of the local church, where the people of God share communion with the one bread and one cup. From the local church the prayer then extends, as in concentric circles, to the universal church so that it too might be strengthened in faith and charity. The horizon widens further by involving the entire world in this prayer and hence embraces the whole of humanity in all its children "wherever they may be."

The force of the Spirit radiating from the bread and wine extends beyond our world to the world of the deceased, who together with us are participating in the eucharist. The term *intercessory prayer* makes us think of prayer said *for* someone. The truest meaning of this part of the eucharistic prayer is rather to pray *with*.

The eucharist is the central celebration of the church whose mysterious power is so great that it penetrates beyond the limits of the church to the entire universe and encompasses also the world of the deceased who are still living branches of the "true vine." So it is a cosmic chorus that rises from the eucharistic table and prepares for that universal praise in which, in that final gathering with the Mother of God, the apostles and saints, and all creatures freed from corruption and sin will be given to the Father in the kingdom of God. The dimension of time is added to the dimension of space, anticipating the moment when the chorus will include the whole of creation in rendering praise to the Father: "Through him, with him, in him, in the unity of the Holy Spirit, all glory and honor are yours for ever and ever."

Our own "Amen" at this point is a recognition and ratification of what is being celebrated. It is the expression of our active presence and represents in that great eschatological song one note that is the object of our waiting and our hope. This song will include an ever-increasing number of voices until the chorus of voices will be the expression of every person and every thing in the entire created world.

THE SIGNS OF UNITY

The character of the eucharist as the "sacrament of unity" is also expressed by the signs of bread and wine. The wheat is composed of many separate grains gathered together to make a single bread. The same is true of the vine from which many grapes of different forms are brought together to make one wine. This was highlighted as early as the writings of Paul:

> The cup of blessing that we bless, is it not a sharing in the blood of Christ? The bread that we break, is it not a sharing in the body of Christ? Because there is one bread, we who are many are one body, for we all partake of the one bread. (1 Corinthians 10:16ff.)

Therefore the unity of the church is created by the one food that nourishes every believer. This is how the ancient church prayed over the broken bread:

> Just as the bread broken
> was first scattered on the hills,
> then was gathered and became one,
> so let your church be gathered
> from the ends of the earth into your kingdom,
> for yours is glory and power through all ages.
> (*The Didache* 9, 4)[9]

This doctrine, whose basis is founded on the evidence of the liturgical sign, is a constant theme in Augustine's sermons. Here is one example:

> Hear, then, in short what the Apostle, or better, what Christ says by the mouth of the Apostle concerning the sacrament of the Lord's table: "We, being many, are one bread, one body." That is all there is to it, as I have quickly summed it up. Yet do not count the words, but rather weigh their meaning; for if you count them they are few, but if you ponder them, their import is tremendous.

> One bread, the apostle said. No matter how many breads were placed before him then, still they were only one bread. No matter how many breads are laid upon the altars of Christ throughout the world today, it is but one bread.

> What is meant by *one bread?* St. Paul interpreted it briefly: "We, being many, are one body." This bread is the body of Christ, to which the Apostle refers when he addresses the church, "Now you are the body of Christ and his members." That which you receive, that you yourselves are by the grace of the redemption, as you acknowledge when you respond "Amen." What you witness here is the sacrament of unity.

> The Apostle has shown us briefly what this bread is. Now consider the matter more carefully and see how it comes about.

How is bread made? Wheat is threshed, ground, moistened and baked. By moistening the wheat is purified, and by baking it is made firm. In what does your threshing consist? You also underwent a form of threshing, by fasting, by the Lenten observances, by night watches, by exorcisms. You were ground when you were delivered from the devil by exorcism. But moistening cannot be done without water; as a consequence, you were immersed. Baking is troublesome yet necessary. What, then, is the baking process? The fire of temptations, from which no life is free. And how is this beneficial? "The furnace trieth the potter's vessels, and the trial of affliction the just." As one loaf results from combining the individual kernels and mixing the same together with water, so also the one body of Christ [the People of God] results from the harmony of love. . . . For wine pours forth from the wine press out of what were formerly many individual grapes now flowing together as one liquid to become wine. Hence both in the bread and in the chalice the sacrament of unity is present." (P.L. Suppl. 11, 554–556)[10]

Up to this point, we have been considering the eucharist as the source of unity among the members of the people of God. Nevertheless, this does not exhaust its unifying power. Not only are all human creatures gathered together and united in the eucharist, but in this sacrament we also encounter both the created world and the world of God, through Christ. In all liturgy, there takes place a healing of the divisions separating human creatures from the material world which was itself created for us. This division, which resulted from sin, is being healed also by our own work, which is gradually subduing nature and enabling it to attain its purpose of being of service to humanity. By means of the work of our own hands, human creatures are reclaiming nature and coming back into harmony with it. We could say that human creatures are slowly *redeeming* the created world by permeating it with their spirit, elevating it to a new level and bringing it to its fulfillment.

Nonetheless, the greatest sublimation of the created world occurs when nature is put in service not only of our natural human life but is also able to serve our supersensible or supernatural life. This happens throughout all of liturgy: For example, water gives us entrance into eternal life and we are consecrated with oil, yet this takes place in the most special way during the eucharist, when the bread and wine become the direct instruments of the real presence of Christ.

In the eucharistic bread and wine we find, as if in concentrated form, all the various levels of life in the universe. There is the world of matter in the wheat and the grapes; there is the presence of the human person whose work has made bread and wine from wheat and grapes, and finally, at the highest level, there is the person of Christ himself, present in his glorious humanity, offered to the Father. The eucharist is the realization of what Paul proclaims: "For all things are yours . . . and you belong to Christ, and Christ belongs to God" (1 Corinthians 3:21ff.).

"All things are yours," and as human persons we take in hand the elements of the created world and put them in service of our needs. Yet "we belong to Christ." Bread and wine have become Christ's body and blood for our nourishment so that, together with Christ and in Christ, we can come to the Father. The entire universe is united in a magnificent synthesis in the eucharist, in which everything is permeated by God's power, a force that penetrates even the depths of inanimate matter, suffusing it all with life and giving it unlimited potentiality so that all can praise the Father.

If liturgy is always the place of encounter between earth and heaven, then the eucharist is the place of encounter *par excellence.* In the eucharist, not only are the worlds of God and the human person united, but also, through us and Christ's mediation, the whole subhuman world is united to the world of God. The eucharist has infinite scope and repercussions in history and in the farthest ranges of the created world: It reaches the very summit of the world.

The Preparation of the Gifts

THE FIRST PART OF THE EUCHARIST HAS LONG BEEN called the *offertory,* a term which owes its name to the fact that it developed around the bringing of the gifts. Throughout the centuries, however, the character of the offertory has changed.

Bringing the gifts, in relation to the eucharist, is documented from earliest times. From Paul we know that originally the eucharist took place during a banquet (1 Corinthians 11:17 – 34). It probably imitated the sacred banquets in use among some groups of devout Jews at the time of Jesus. In this case, everyone had to bring something for the meal. We also know from the same text of Paul that there were frequent abuses in this custom, and soon a separation of the eucharist from the banquet had to be effected.

In the First Apologia (65 – 67) of Justin, a Christian apologist of the second century to whom we owe the oldest text providing information on the rite of the Mass, it is no longer spoken of as a banquet. He says only that they used to bring gifts for the needs of the poor. The bringing of gifts has changed in character: It is no longer dictated by the needs of the banquet but becomes a manifestation of charity toward the community, an expression of an interior attitude that is necessary for participation in the eucharist.

The bringing of gifts takes on a ritual form between the fourth and seventh centuries. It is the Roman liturgy that makes it a part of the liturgical action and gives it the importance of a true and proper rite. The rite is made up of two elements: a song accompanying the procession of the faithful who bring their gifts to the altar, and a prayer (our prayer over the gifts) with which the priest concludes the action of the faithful and the sanctifying of the gifts. The offering is therefore closely connected to communion.

Since the ninth century, the offertory has been increasingly reserved for the priest. The introduction of unleavened bread made the bringing of the bread more difficult for the faithful, who were gradually distanced also from this part of the Mass. The focus shifts toward the priest's gestures; each of his gestures is accompanied by a prayer and concludes by attributing to them the meaning of the gestures of offering.

The offertory thus becomes a type of duplicate canon: Both the prayers and the form of the offertory closely resemble the canon. This is not without some drawbacks, since there is the risk of diverting attention from the essential moment of the Mass, making the offertory almost an entity in itself that is not in close connection to the canon, almost dividing the sacrifice into our sacrifice on one side and Christ's sacrifice on the other. There is a danger, then, of losing the understanding that there is only one sacrifice, the sacrifice of Christ. Every offering made on our part must pass through Christ to reach the Father, must be offered with Christ and in Christ.

In the Missal that dates from 1969 and is the fruit of the liturgical reform of the Second Vatican Council, the offertory is presented as the "Preparation of the Gifts," and the term "offertory" has been dropped (see the sacramentary). The form in some ways bears traces of the first part of the blessing of the table in Jewish liturgy, thereby expressing itself primarily as thanksgiving to God for the gift of bread and wine. The washing of the hands is also found in the Jewish liturgy of the preparation and blessing of the table.

The offertory nature of the sacrifice has been retained in the second part. There we ask to be received as "humble and contrite" and that our sacrifice may be pleasing to God. Moreover, in the dialogue that introduces the prayer over the offerings, it is the offertory aspect of the sacrifice which is the focus. In summary, the "Preparation of the Gifts" now presents a composite character in the Roman Missal.

The Liturgy of the Word

THE LITURGY OF THE WORD IS DISTINCT FROM THE eucharist by its nature and origin. The eucharist is the sacrifice that actualizes salvation; the liturgy of the word proclaims that salvation is present here and now. As we have seen, the origin of the eucharist in its ritual form will be found in the Jewish Passover banquet. The origin of the liturgy of the word will be found in synagogue worship, which centered on the word of God in scripture — in particular the Torah, the first five books of the Bible and the most sacred for the Jews — and on prayer as the response of the human person to God's word.

The synagogue is distinct from the Temple. There was only one Temple, in Jerusalem. The Temple was built to preserve the Ark of the Covenant and the tablets of the Torah, which constitute the presence of God. When speaking of the place of the presence of God, it is clear that one cannot conceive of more than one. Destroyed the first time in 586 BC, the Temple was rebuilt at the end of the exile. In the innermost area of the new Temple, which was the most sacred, there was nothing, since the Ark had been destroyed.

When the Romans broke into the Temple in AD 70, they were astonished to find an environment devoid of statues of the divinity. Imperial temples, full of idols, were not surrounded by such veneration as this incredibly empty space! The Temple, the dwelling place of the presence of God, was also the seat of bloody sacrifice, the worship that could not be performed without a priesthood.

From the time of the Babylonian exile, a new spirituality developed in Israel whose hinge, or turning point, was the Torah, a word we customarily translate inadequately as Law, thereby attributing a legal meaning to it. Instead, the Torah is for the Jews the teaching *par excellence,* the teaching of God that, inasmuch as it is the expression of God's will, has normative value as well.

Since the exile, Israel, deprived of its Temple, centered its religious life on the Torah and on the human person's response to it, namely, prayer. In this way, a spirituality developed that tended to separate itself from the Temple and the caste that presided there, in order to become the spirituality of the whole people of Israel. All Israel becomes a priestly people. One speaks of the "sacrifice of the lips," the prayer that is affirmed to be more pleasing to God than bloody worship. A spirituality of this kind is not tied solely to the contingent causes of the exile; in fact, it continues and develops even after the reconstruction of the Temple. This spirituality will find its center in the synagogue, which is set up with a certain polemic intent toward the Temple. The survival and prospering of Israel as a religious group after the destruction of the second Temple is due to the synagogue.

We know that worship in the synagogue gradually made the reading of the Torah its nucleus and eventually included the reading of the prophets. This second reading was sometimes a passage that in a narrative and historical form was more or less explanatory of the first. At other times, it offered a rereading of the first passage in an eschatological key. Synagogue worship, then, seems to us dynamically oriented toward the waiting for the future.

An element that was definitely constant in pre-Christian synagogue worship was the *qaddish*, a prayer we could call the twin of the "Our Father":

> Magnified and sanctified be his great Name in the world which he hath created according to his will. May he establish his kingdom during your life and during your days, and during the life of all the house of Israel, even speedily and at a near time. . . .[11]

This is essentially a messianic prayer oriented toward the waiting for the Messiah, praying that he might come soon in our time. What is of utmost interest for us is the fact that Jesus solemnly proclaims precisely during worship in the synagogue that he is the Messiah. The fact is not accidental. Jesus, who assiduously attended the synagogue, knew that in the synagogue he would find the most suitable environment, in the actual and moral sense, in which to proclaim his message.

The Gospel of Luke has preserved a passage that we could define as the first Christian liturgy of the word (4:16ff). This worship took place in the synagogue in Nazareth where Jesus went on a Sabbath at the very moment when he began his public life. There he is called on to explain to those present (according to the custom of choosing someone from the congregation who might be able to explain the scripture) a text of Isaiah (chapter 61) in which it is the Messiah himself who speaks in the first person:

> The spirit of the LORD God is upon me, because the LORD has anointed me; he has sent me to bring good news to the oppressed. . . . to proclaim liberty to the captives, and release to the prisoners; to proclaim the year of the LORD's favor.

We do not know if this passage was chosen by Jesus or suggested to him. Yet in the course of explaining this text, Jesus said that it was being fulfilled in him: The mysterious Messiah, object of so much expectancy and such hope, now has a face and a name. This does not mean that the waiting is over, because we are waiting for the completion of his work; we are awaiting his "coming" when "all the nations will be gathered before him" (Matthew 25:32). Nonetheless, a great step in the advance of history has been accomplished.

Just as Jesus did at Nazareth, so his apostles continued to do. Even Paul, known as the Apostle to the Gentiles, always begins his preaching in the synagogues. Paul was a Jew; when he entered a foreign city, he would obviously look for the place most natural to him. The synagogue represented for the Apostle to the Gentiles exactly the place most related to him by origin, but it was also and above all the most suitable place to follow Jesus' example by proclaiming the presence of the Messiah.

As for the oldest form of the liturgy of the word, the facts are scarce. At times the liturgy of the word would take place in the synagogues, at other times on the Sabbath (see for example, Acts 13:5, 14, 44; 14:1; 16:13; 17:1, 10, and others) or in private homes, evidently in the homes of the first Christians. What is narrated in Acts 20:7ff. already takes place outside synagogue worship: It is Sunday, and the word is now closely connected to the "breaking of bread," namely, the eucharist. We can recognize here the actual structure of Christian worship: The liturgy of the word is the introduction to the eucharist, which actualizes the word proclaimed. In other words, the first part of the Mass announces the salvation that is present in the person of Jesus, and in the eucharist, salvation is accomplished in the reactualization of the paschal event. Consequently, even in apostolic times the two parts of the Mass, while distinct from each other, appear linked.

The oldest outline of the Mass is preserved in a text by Justin Martyr, a second-century apologist:

> On the day of sun, all those who live in the city and the country assemble together in the same place. They read the memoirs of the apostles and writings of the prophets. When the lector has finished, the one who is presiding then begins to speak and to admonish those present. Then we all rise to our feet and lift up our voices in prayer.

From this text it seems that the readings were taken from the Old Testament (the "writings of the prophets") and from the New Testament ("the memoirs of the apostles" are the epistles or letters, but primarily the gospel). Therefore, even though the liturgy of the word has since changed several times, it has preserved the structure of synagogue worship until today, with the addition of the new element, the gospel message.

In Justin's text, it seems that there was no preparatory rite; the liturgy began immediately with the readings and commentary. In Augustine's time too, the Mass began directly with the readings: "We proceeded toward the people; the church was full of voices and people who were acclaiming. I greeted the people. When all became silent, the sacred scriptures were solemnly read." However, the *Didache* (14:1, 2) speaks of the confession of sins. The recitation of the "Confiteor" probably derived from monastic custom and was introduced into the Roman Mass in the eleventh century.

1. J. Jeremias, *Le Parole dell'Ultima Cena* (Brescia: 1967), 230.

2. J. Jeremias, op. cit., 233; J. Carmignac, *La Nascita dei Vangeli Sinottici* (Ed. Paoline, 1975), 74.

3. S. Marsili, "Il 'Triduo Sacro' e il Giovedì Santo," in *Rivista Liturgica* (1968, I): 37.

4. Lucien Deiss, "The Apostolic Tradition," in *Springtime of the Liturgy* (Collegeville, MN: The Liturgical Press), 130-131.

5. Lucien Deiss, "The Apostolic Constitutions," in *Springtime of the Liturgy,* 232 – 234.

6. M.Righetti, *Storia Liturgica*, vol. 3 (Milano: 1956), 343ff.

7. J.H. McKenna, "The Eucharistic Epiclesis," in *Ephemerides Liturgicae* (1976) 3 – 4, pp. 289 – 326; 5 – 6, pp. 446 – 482. From the same, "Eucharist and Holy Spirit, Great Awakening" (1975).

8. M.Righetti, *Storia Liturgica*, 376ff.

9. Lucien Deiss, *Springtime of the Liturgy,* 75.

10. Philip T. Weller, *Selected Easter Sermons of St. Augustine,* "On the Eucharist – Easter Sunday" (B. Herder Book Co.: 1959), 101 – 102.

11. Carmine DiSante, *Jewish Prayer: The Origins of Christian Liturgy,* trans. M.J. O'Connell (New Jersey: Paulist Press, 1985), 171.

Sacraments of Healing

RESTORE US TO YOURSELF, O LORD,

THAT WE MAY BE RESTORED.

LAMENTATIONS 5:21

The Sacrament of Reconciliation

WE CANNOT SPEAK ABOUT THE SACRAMENT OF reconciliation without addressing, if only in passing, the problem of sin. Our religious life can be thought of as a dialogue between God and the human person, a dialogue that God initiates and that calls forth a response from us. The entire history of salvation is basically this dialogue: God speaks to us, offers us gifts, and we respond (or do not respond) to God's word and accept (or do not accept) God's gifts. With this twofold movement from heaven to earth and earth to heaven, a bond is established between God and us, a bond which in biblical language is called *covenant* (pact, testament). But whereas God's act of self-giving in the covenant is constant and faithful, our response is not always as constant and faithful.

Even at the beginning of the world, Adam answers "no" to God's self-offering. And so, throughout the history of salvation, the response of the Jewish people is sometimes adequate, sometimes not. The same must be said of the church of Christ. Thus sin is introduced into the world. The Old Testament has three words to indicate sin. The first word we can translate as "rebellion." This applies to sin primarily in the context of the covenant, in which the lesser contracting party, the human person, *breaks the faithfulness* due the more eminent contracting party, God. The second term corresponds to the word "iniquity" and points to sin as *deviation,* something that, instead of making us walk the right path that leads to God, diverts us from our true path and makes us proceed by winding ways. The third word corresponds to "deficiency" or "lack" and sees sin as the lack of a goal or aim, as *missing the mark.*

However, the commitment God has made in the covenant remains steadfast even toward man and woman, who have fallen into a state of degradation. For instance, in Ezekiel 16, Israel is described as a young woman, born in the desert, to whom no one has given the most rudimentary care and who is left abandoned to wallow in her own blood. But the Lord, passing by and seeing that "you were the age for love," enters into a covenant of betrothal with Israel. He adorns her with costly garments and precious jewels and makes her fit to be a queen whose fame spreads among the nations and whose beauty is perfect "because of my splendor that I had bestowed on you" (Ezekiel 16:14). Thus the sudden transformation from a forsaken young woman to a veritable queen comes as a gift from God and through God's love.

The source and point of departure in the covenant remains always with God, but God's initiative calls forth a corresponding action on our part. "Restore us to yourself, O Lord, that we may be restored" (Lamentations 5:21). The inner stirring to come back, that is, to repentance, comes to us from God; it is incumbent upon us to accept God's promptings within us. So too the sacrament of reconciliation consists of an action on God's part and an action on our part.

God is the source of the process of *conversion.* It is God's constancy in love, God's tireless calling of the sheep, that gradually changes our hearts and brings us to confess our sins. By listening to the voice of God, by coming face to face with God's word, we become aware of our deficiencies and needs, and we feel the inner stirring to become different, better, to be more "light in the Lord" (Ephesians 5:8).

The conversion process becomes a reality in the encounter with God through the sacrament of reconciliation, administered by a priest of the church. Inasmuch as they are addressed to God, the words we speak to the confessor are prayer above all else. The prayer of confession presents various aspects. It is prayer of repentance. Augustine, in speaking of this aspect, says that through repentance one begins to unite oneself to God so that God's perspective and judgment become one's own. As we begin to be displeased by what displeases God, we will come to hate what God hates. Sinners, Augustine says, have spoiled God's image in themselves: "Having become unlike God, you look at yourself and you don't like yourself; you begin then to become like him because what displeases God displeases you" (*Expositions on the Psalms* 8, 15). Repentance is the movement whereby the human creature begins to respond to God's initiative in the conversion process. If this point is stressed too much, to the detriment of others, it can lead to an over-emphasis on the psychological aspect and, more importantly, it can overshadow God's action by giving too much weight to our part in the process of conversion.

Moreover, if we were to focus only on this one aspect of the prayer of confession, we would make the sacrament an act that is turned toward the past alone. Rather, this sacrament is a new step on the path toward that fullness of life that God wants for each one of us. Therefore, confession is also a prayer of petition that our emptiness will be filled with God's love, that our weakness will be strengthened with the gift of the Holy Spirit, that our darkness will be illumined with God's light. In confessing our faults, we are asking that God's "power is made perfect in weakness" (2 Corinthians 12:9ff). Thus, confession is also a petitionary prayer.

Confession is a prayer of repentance and a prayer of petition, but most of all it is a prayer of praise. "We confess," says Augustine,

> both when we praise God and when we accuse ourselves. Both confessions belong to "mercy," whether you correct yourself, you who are not without sin, or whether you praise the One who cannot sin. . . . In confession, accusing oneself is praising God. . . . When we praise God, we proclaim him as One who is without sin; when we accuse ourselves, we give thanks to him through whom we are brought back to life. *(Expositions on the Psalms)*

Augustine affirms that without this aspect of praise of God, confession is not a religious act.

> When one confesses one's own sins, one must confess them by praising God, and in order to be religious, the confession of sins must be without despair and must ask for God's mercy. Thus it contains praise of God, both in words, when we proclaim that He is good and merciful, and even in sentiment alone, when we believe that He is like that. . . . One cannot praise God in a true and devout manner without the confession of sins; but, there is no devout and profitable confession if God is not praised, whether with the heart, or with the mouth and words." (*Expositions on the Psalms* 105, 2)

The operative action of God is realized and expressed in the sacramental signs of the imposition, or laying on, of hands (*cheirotonia*), with the sign of the cross, and with the words of absolution with which the confessor "looses" or unbinds (absolution comes from *absolvo*, "I loose") the penitent from those chains that impede the full and free use of one's capabilities. With the gesture of the laying on of hands, the Father is asked to give the power of the Holy Spirit. The gesture of the sign of the cross, sign of Christ's victory over evil, covers us like a shield with which to defend ourselves in the struggle against evil.

The penitent leaves the sacrament of reconciliation reinvigorated and able to look to the future with more trust. That branch that baptism grafted onto Christ, the true vine, that branch that had impeded the flow of sap into itself and so made it appear less luxuriant, once more receives the divine sap in abundance that will make it capable of bearing fruit.

The work that the penitent accepts to do is, yes, a desire to annul the errors made, and as such it is an expression of repentance and reparation. Yet perhaps it is first and foremost the first step on the path of *coming back,* an expression of the new life that the sacrament has given us. The traditional works of penance are almsgiving, fasting and prayer.

LITURGICAL HISTORY OF CONFESSION

From the gospel we know that Jesus forgave sins and that he cared for sinners in a special way, something that caused scandal among the respectable or well thought of. To these Jesus replied that "it is not the healthy who need the doctor, but the sick." This special attitude of Jesus emerges in both the numerous deeds recounted in the gospel as well as in the parables of the lost sheep, the lost coin and the prodigal son (Luke 15). The first two parables especially emphasize the fact that the return of the sinner concerns not only the believer and God but is also a festive celebration for the whole community. Both the shepherd who has found his sheep and the woman who has found the coin call their friends to rejoice and celebrate a feast with them.

We know that Jesus' miracles were manifestations of his divine power, and Jesus reveals his power to forgive sins, in particular through the healing of the paralytic at Capernaum (Matthew 9). On that occasion the physical healing was worked for the purpose of convincing those present, through a mighty visible deed, of the wondrous, invisible work Jesus had effected in the soul of the sick man by forgiving his sins. In the soul of each repentant and forgiven sinner something takes place on the spiritual level that corresponds on a physical level to the healing of a sickness that limits one's possibilities. Just as sin limits the interior capacities of the one who is created in the image of God, so does God's forgiveness confer, once again, the life-giving vitality of divine life.

Jesus has left his power to the church. He promises it to Peter, after the disciple acknowledges that Jesus is the Son of God, with the words:

> Blessed are you, Simon son of Jonah! For flesh and blood
> has not revealed this to you, but my Father in heaven.
> And I tell you, you are Peter, and on this rock I will build my
> church. . . . I will give you the keys of the kingdom of
> heaven, and whatever you bind on earth will be bound in

heaven, and whatever you loose on earth will be loosed in
heaven. (Matthew 16: 17 – 19)

Again, speaking to all the disciples, he repeats the promise:
"Truly I tell you, whatever you bind on earth will be bound in
heaven, and whatever you loose on earth will be loosed in
heaven" (Matthew 18:18).

    The power to loose and to bind is conferred on Easter
evening. Redemption has been accomplished, and the risen
Jesus appears to the apostles, saying: "Peace be with you." Jesus
shows them his wounds and says again: "Peace be with you.
As the Father has sent me, so I send you." Having said this, Jesus
breathes on them and says: "Receive the Holy Spirit. If you
forgive the sins of any, they are forgiven them; if you retain the
sins of any, they are retained" (John 20:21). Breath is one of
the signs by which the Holy Spirit is transmitted, and the meaning of this gesture is then explained in words. Jesus promises
the gift of the Holy Spirit to make it understood that he is trans-
mitting a power of salvation to the apostles that will be exercised
by means of the Holy Spirit. It is because of this power that the
apostles can forgive and retain sins.

    In ancient penitential practices, three conditions were
required of the penitent: confession, public penance and
absolution. The earliest sources are not very clear on the practice
of confession. It has been ascertained, at any rate, that confession was made to the bishop and in private. Acceptance of a
public penance was already an explicit confession of grave sin
in that it was given only for especially evident failings. Such
penances consisted of long and serious privations and humilia-
tions, most importantly the exclusion from Mass, which marked
one's official entrance in the order of penitents. This is why it
was called *excommunicatio*, namely, exclusion from the communion table, the source of life in common. The *excommunicatio*,
or penance, had a limited duration: In Paul (1 Corinthians
5:1ff.) we read that a man guilty of incest was to be "handed over
to Satan" and then reconciled, that is, readmitted to communion.

In this way it was clear that the eucharist was the goal of penance and that there was a healing purpose in being deprived of it. Indeed, Paul says in reference to some blasphemers: "I have turned [them] over to Satan, so that they may learn not to blaspheme" (1 Timothy 1:20). Tertullian lists a series of acts to expiate sins, and says that among other things:

> One is obliged to present oneself in a humbled, disorderly state, to be drowned in painful sadness, to transform with hard treatment the inclinations leading to fault, and, as for food and drink, to keep to a strict regimen to maintain life, not to satisfy the stomach.

Moreover, one must:

> moan day and night, calling upon your Lord God; drag yourself in front of the presbyters; go down on your knees before people dear to God and entrust oneself to the intercession of the prayers of all the brethren.

In the East, three categories of penitents are spoken of: the listeners *(auditores)*, that is, those who could be present only at the first part of the Mass (liturgy of the word); the genuflectors, those who could assist at the whole Mass on the condition that they remained kneeling; and the assistants, so-called because their humiliation was to assist at Mass without being able to receive communion. According to some sources, there was a fourth category, the mourners, who would represent those who were in mourning. The sins that were considered deserving of public penitence were reduced to three: idolatry, murder and adultery. Less serious faults were not submitted to any particular discipline.

Reconciliation took place in front of the community. Sin is a fact that concerns the whole community, which is harmed by the poor conduct of one of its members. Reconciliation also is a communal fact, since the whole community of believers enjoys the return of the sinners and ought to help them come back with its prayers. This aspect is not very evident in current penitential practices, whereas it was quite clear in the early church. Reconciliation was a solemn, public rite during which the bishop and college of presbyters placed their hands on the penitents and readmitted them to the ranks of the faithful and to communion. Thus, from being outside the community (*excommunicatio*) one returned to the community (*communio*) in a rite that had an obvious communal nature. St. Jerome says:

> The priest makes the offering for the layman; he lays his hands on him, calls on the Holy Spirit to return, so that he who was handed over to Satan for the mortification of the flesh, by public announcement before all the people, might be reconciled to the altar. But a member is not reinstated in holiness until all the members have prayed for him; in fact, the father easily forgives the son when the mother (the church) prays through the fruit of her womb.

Thus, reconciliation took place in front of the whole church. In time, public penance was relegated to the period of Lent, and then reconciliation was assigned to Holy Thursday. Soon the custom of considering Lent as a penitential period for the whole church took root, and those who had not fallen into serious sin would also dedicate this period in particular to fasting, almsgiving and prayer.

There are frequent allusions to baptism in the liturgy of reconciliation. The sacrament of reconciliation is considered almost a renewed baptism, inasmuch as both sacraments obtain the forgiveness of sins. For instance, in the formulary of reconciliation contained in the eighth-century Gelasian sacramentary, the deacon presents to the bishop the penitents who have prostrated themselves, saying: "waters wash clean, tears [of repentance] wash clean. From the first, the chosen one's joy of arrival, from the second, the penitent's happiness in absolution."

Another example is the following, an early prayer of reconciliation:

> Remember, O most merciful Lord, with your customary goodness, these your servants whom sin has separated from

you, for you heard Peter's sobs and entrusted to him the keys of the kingdom. Accept then, O Lord most merciful, these people for whom we offer you our prayers and bring them back to the bosom of the church, so that the enemy may not triumph in any way in them, but let your son, who is equal to you, reconcile them to you, purify them of every fault so that they may be worthy to be admitted to the eucharistic banquet. May he restore them with his flesh and blood in order to lead them, after the course of this life, to the Kingdom of Heaven!

PRIVATE PENANCE

From relatively ancient times, the practice of private penance took place side by side with public penance, but without ever replacing it. There are those who say that private penance originated in what they used to call "spiritual therapy" (today we would call it "spiritual direction"), which was already known in the earliest years of the church (Clement and Origen knew of it). It was a matter of opening one's conscience to a person known for their spirituality, including a lay person, who would become a guide in the spiritual life. This "therapy" was recommended, and by the fourth century it was widespread in monastic environments in the East. The rule of St. Basil contributed a great deal to spreading it, pointing to the head of the community, whether priest or lay person, as the doctor of the soul.

That it spread to lay people is probably due to the Irish monks who, in the sixth century, began to bring even to the laity something of the austerity of the monastery. The extension of this practice to the laity began first in Irish circles, but fired by a missionary spirit, the monks soon left their country and went to England and later to the continent. One of the most famous of these monks was St. Columban, who died in 615. On the continent, torn asunder by barbarian invasions, the work of spiritual renewal carried out by the monks was extremely advantageous.

What was private penance? We read in some texts that both clergy and lay persons went to their own confessors; when the confessor had heard the confession, a penance would be imposed. Up to this point there is nothing different from public penance. What is new here is the fact that the penance, even though it was sometimes hard, was carried out not in sight of the community but in private. Moreover, in Ireland originated the practice of giving absolution immediately following confession, before the penance has been performed. But the greater novelty is that people began to confess minor sins as well. This was a clear sign of the refining of one's conscience. In the ninth century, Alcuin recommended that even "the most minute" faults be confessed.

In relation to this, an important fact in the liturgical history of the sacrament is the change in the name of the sacrament that begins to be recorded in the late Middle Ages: Instead of speaking of penance, the people started speaking of "confession." In the phenomenon of changing a name, there is always something profound that goes beyond the name itself. If a name changes, it means that something has changed in the very structure of the institution.

In reference to this sacrament, such a change shows that people began to consider the humiliation represented by the confession of one's own faults as a sacrifice *(confessionis sacrificium)* sufficient to replace entirely or in part the burdensome public penance. This concept was later made clearer in the age of scholasticism: Confession took the foreground, and penance moved to second place. After this time, there was the problem of how often to confess, and confession of venial sins became more widespread. In particular, prominence was given to confession at the beginning of Lent, the period when the members of the Christian community were called to become aware of their own sinful condition. The need to be redeemed from that state of course required confession.

Nonetheless, there was no immediate uniformity in penitential practices, and cases of public penance, concerning mostly public sins, remained side-by-side with private penance. Thus the precept was instituted that public penance correspond to public sins, private penance to private sins. The Lateran Council in 1215 established the practice of confession for children as well, and even fixed the age for boys at 14 and for girls at 12. Yearly confession was made to the parish priest as a substitute for the bishop. A legal character was given to the secrecy of the confessional, an aspect which was already recognized in the actual practice of the sacrament. Finally, the arrival of private penance overshadowed the communal nature of the sacrament that was so evident in early penitential practices.

The new term currently used to indicate the sacrament is *reconciliation*. This term highlights the context of the covenant in which the believer lives, the relationship one has diminished by sinning. The sacrament is to reconcile us with God and with the church, which, as we mentioned, is harmed by the sin of its members and which joins with sinners so as to help them in their return, their coming back.

Anointing of the Sick

THE ANOINTING OF THE SICK HAS A CHARACTER ALL its own among the seven sacraments. It is called "the medicine of the church" *(medicina ecclesiae),* and it is the sacrament that is aligned with reconciliation in cases of serious illness. The Council of Trent defined it as the perfection of penance in that it removes all residue of sin. It is exactly because it is a means for removing all trace of sin that it resembles reconciliation. It differs from reconciliation, however, in that it takes away only venial sin and is not based on any external manifestation of guilt. In the anointing of the sick, there is no confession in the strict sense of the word; that is, those receiving it are not asked to specify their sins. There is another element that further differentiates it from reconciliation: The sacrament of anointing is oriented to a physical effect as well, the effect of healing. It is in the nature of the sacrament of anointing to seek, to aim for, and very often to attain, healing on the physical level. This is not found, at least in an explicit way, in the other sacraments.

The healing obtained as a result of the anointing should not be considered a miracle but rather a manifestation on the physical level of spiritual well-being, inasmuch as the supernatural effect is reflected also on the physical plane. In the miracle Jesus performed on the paralytic man in Capernaum, two miraculous deeds can be discerned: the forgiveness of sins and the physical healing. In the anointing of the sick, however, there is only one sacramental act, and it can have two distinct results: the spiritual result, which is infallible, and the physical, toward which the sacrament by its nature is oriented and many times obtains. In fact, this sacrament is for the healing of the whole person, body and soul; it also indicates both earthly and heavenly health. As such it has an eschatological dimension as well.

ILLNESS AND SIN

In order to understand the connection between illness and sin in this sacrament, we must refer to the biblical concept of illness. It is undisputed that the Bible presents a connection between sickness and sin in the sense that sickness entered the world as a consequence of sin. In Genesis we read that the Lord said to Adam as punishment for the sin committed: "You shall die!" And indeed, death is the ultimate physical diminishment. The relationship between illness and sin is actual and real, but this is true only in a general sense, since very rarely is it possible to determine a direct relationship between a certain illness and a certain sin: The reality of sickness is tied to the fact that sin entered the world.

In the book of Job, we see that even the just person can become ill. Satan had God's permission to tempt Job, who was a just man; how would he react to the test? Forbidden to at first, Job later protests his innocence in a vigorous way, affirming that he does not deserve such affliction. The book admits, then, that there is the possibility that a just person may suffer, which means that the reason for the suffering of an innocent person is not in the person but in the fallen state of the human race.

The disciples, referring to the man who was blind from birth, ask: "Master, since he was born blind, who sinned, this man or his parents?" Jesus replies: "Neither this man nor his parents sinned" (John 9:3). The man is blind because blindness is one of the miseries that came into the world with sin; but this particular fact is not explained on the basis of the personal, actual failings of an individual person.

The Messiah is the new Adam, and as such he will repair the damage set loose in the world by the first Adam. If then the first Adam unleashed sickness and death in this world, the new Adam will remedy sickness and overcome death. If sickness is connected to sin, so healing will be connected to the messianic work of Jesus.

The prophets had already proclaimed that in the messianic era there would be miraculous healings: "Then the eyes of the blind shall be opened, and the ears of the deaf unstopped; then the lame shall leap like a deer, and the tongue of the speechless sing for joy" (Isaiah 35:5 – 6). Miraculous healings will be characteristic of the messianic era. Indeed, when John the Baptist is being held in prison and sends his disciples to Jesus to find out if he is the one who is to come, Jesus answers: "Go and tell John what you hear and see: the blind receive their sight, the lame walk, the lepers are cleansed, the deaf hear" (Matthew 11:4ff.). If the miraculous healings foretold by the prophets are being worked, this means that the messianic era has arrived, and if the source of these healings is Jesus, it is clear that he must be the Messiah.

This promise will not amaze us if we rediscover the connection between healing and forgiveness in the sacrament of anointing. The sacrament reproduces in a particular way the function fulfilled by Jesus in this world. The twofold nature of the effects — spiritual and physical — that derive from the sacrament of anointing repeat what Jesus did during his earthly life: Jesus healed and forgave. The church inherits from him the power to heal and to forgive.

SOURCES CONCERNING
THE SACRAMENT OF ANOINTING

The oldest text concerning the anointing is a passage from the letter of James (5:14ff.), which is contained in the rite itself:

> Are any among you sick? They should call for the elders of the church and have them pray over them, anointing them with oil in the name of the Lord. The prayer of faith will save the sick and the Lord will raise them up; and anyone who has committed sins will be forgiven.

James's text reflects the Judeo-Christian liturgy of the mother church. Even in a text as early as this, the necessity for a priestly ministry is emphasized. In the prayer said "over him" (the sick person) we see an allusion to the laying on of hands that accompanies the anointing with oil in the present rite. The double effect of the sacrament is clearly indicated: "He will raise him up" alludes to the physical well-being which the sacrament can bring, and the forgiveness of sins is explicitly stated.

It is during the Carolingian epoch (ninth century and later) that, through a misunderstood spirituality, the curative capabilities of the sacrament tended to be overshadowed, emphasizing instead its spiritual powers. The Council of Trent specified that the sacrament of anointing frees us from venial sin, from the weakness caused by sin, and also gives health to the body. The doctrine of the double effect of the sacrament is also found in the current rite of anointing. One of the prayers that follows the anointing says:

> Lord Jesus Christ, our Redeemer,
> by the grace of your Holy Spirit
> cure the weakness of your servants.
> Heal their sickness and forgive their sins;
> expel all afflictions of mind and body;
> mercifully restore them to full health,
> and enable them to resume their former duties,
> for you are Lord for ever and ever.
> (*Pastoral Care of the Sick,* 142b)

Sacramental Signs

NOW WE HAVE RECEIVED

NOT THE SPIRIT OF THE WORLD,

BUT THE SPIRIT THAT IS FROM GOD,

SO THAT WE MAY UNDERSTAND

THE GIFTS BESTOWED ON US BY GOD.

1 CORINTHIANS 2:12

The Sign of the Cross

IN THE ESSENTIAL MOMENT OF EACH SACRAMENT,
we will always find the sign of the cross, the symbol of salvation.
Given the importance of this sign in the church's liturgy, it is
necessary to know its significance. Today, we tend to think of
the cross primarily as an instrument of Christ's passion and
suffering. It is usually the image of Christ dying or dead on the
cross that we see. This concept of the cross comes later in
history and is due to the influence of an ascetic spirituality that
tended to emphasize the negative elements of renunciation
and suffering, obscuring the fundamental fact that renunciation
and suffering are necessary instruments of the resurrection.

Quite different is the concept of the cross that is found
in paleo-Christian texts. There the cross is the sign of the
universality of Christ's power. The four points, or extremities, of
the cross are thought of in this sense: the saving power of Christ
reaches up to the heights (into the world of angels) and
penetrates into the depths (to the world of the dead); it extends
outward east and west, north and south.

The power of the cross is so universal that Justin
(second century) sees it reflected in many objects of daily life:

> Reflect and see if anything on earth can exist without this
> sign: It is the basis of everything. Can we cleave the sea if this
> trophy called a mast was not raised on a ship? Can one
> plough without the cross? Can the laborer work without tools
> that appear in that shape? We humans only differ in appear-
> ance from animals because we stand erect and can stretch
> out our arms (thus taking on the shape of the cross), and
> even the prominent nose, organ of life-giving breath, traces a
> cross in the middle of the face. You will see still more signs

that express the power of the cross. I mean the banners and trophies that point out that the cross is the sign of your power and strength.

The mystery of the cross is thus hidden in every sphere of nature: Justin does not point out the anchor, which is a frequent symbol of the cross, nor the bird, whose outspread wings draw a cross on the sky. So we can say that we find the sign of the cross on the surface and in the depths of the sea, on land and in the heights of the sky. Judeo-Christians were alluding to the universality of the power of the cross when they surrounded the cross with a circle or square that represented the universe.

The cross is often identified with the risen Christ and is considered living. It is said that Christ rose from the cross and ascends into heaven; the cross is Christ in the mystery of his person and the symbol of his salvific strength. The cross is also a prophetic sign of the parousia. The "sign of the Son of Man" is interpreted by the Fathers as the sign of the cross, and therefore it is a luminous cross that precedes the glorified Christ.

In order to understand the meaning and scope of the sacraments that nourish our Christian life, we need to redis-cover the universal and eschatological dimension of the cross, which is present at the essential moment of each sacrament. Then we will see in the cross the sign of the actualization, now in time, of the presence of the glorified Christ in the world and in the lives of his believers, and in the cross we will see a concrete sign of the anticipation of the Messiah who will return.

The Liturgical Year

THE LITURGICAL YEAR BEGINS WITH THE PREPARA-
tion for Christmas: Advent. There does, however, remain a trace
of a beginning of the liturgical year that coincided with the
start of the Easter cycle. The Liturgy of the Hours (Divine Office)
begins with the reading from Genesis 1:1ff in the week that
used to be called *Septuagesima,* that is, three weeks before Lent.
The church's liturgical year has inherited many elements from
the liturgy of the synagogue. Both are divided into two cycles,
spring and autumn, each cycle being based on the major feasts
of each season. In addition, the celebrations of each cycle show
similarities in structure and sometimes in spirit.

THE CHRISTMAS-EPIPHANY CYCLE

The Christmas cycle has many points in common with the
Jewish autumn cycle. Comparing them will help us to
understand better the messianic character of the Christian cycle
of Christmas, which is being rather lost now in order to give
place to a feast that is understood more as a commemoration of
the historical fact of Jesus' birth in the flesh. The Christmas
cycle is completed with the feast of the Epiphany, and both
feasts must be considered, as the cycle intended, to implore and
celebrate the Messiah's coming in glory at the end of time.

The Jewish Heritage The Jewish autumn cycle is quite complex.
There are three different celebrations: New Year's Day, the Day
of Atonement, and the Feast of the Tabernacles. While form-
ing one cycle, each feast has its own particular character. New
Year's Day is the feast when the Lord judges the people and decides
the destiny of each person. The Jewish greeting exchanged on
New Year's evening is "good seal," which means: "May the Lord
place a good seal on your fate in this new year that has started."
Thus it is a feast of renewal, when the world returns to its original

state, but on a higher plane: On New Year's Day the people wait for the coming of the messiah, who will renew all things.

But the Day of Atonement, which comes shortly afterward, already begins to cast its shadow: At dawn on New Year's Day, the Jews begin to invoke God's forgiveness of their sins. Between the first beginning of the world and the concluding moment of the return of the messiah, there is another renewal, that of the people of Israel today, through repentance.

The Jewish New Year is preceded by seven sabbaths of preparation that have a twofold character: penitential and messianic, linked to the concept that the messiah comes at the New Year. For four of these weeks (the number corresponds to our period of Advent), special prayers are prescribed; these prayers are called "pardons" because they call on God to pardon. Among the biblical readings at the synagogue during this period, there is the text of Isaiah 40:1, which begins: "Comfort, O comfort my people, says your God. Speak tenderly to Jerusalem." It is the same text in which we read: "Make straight in the desert a highway for our God," which has a clearly messianic character. Then there is Isaiah 60:1ff: "Arise, shine; for your light has come." Jerusalem is invited to keep her gates open night and day, so great will be the wealth of nations coming to her.

The preparation for Christmas also has a messianic and penitential character. The name "advent" originally had a marked messianic significance and points to the return of Christ at the end of the world *(parousia)*. This messianic character is reflected in the church's readings during Advent, when the church, like the synagogue, reads Isaiah 40; on the feast of the Epiphany we read Isaiah 60. The reference to the Messiah emerges quite clearly from many prayers that are part of this cycle as well.

In conclusion, there is a whole series of elements common to Christmas, Epiphany and the Jewish New Year as well as the periods that prepare for them. All of this can hardly be accidental; rather, it is a testimony to their common source, an inheritance passed on to the church from the synagogue. This will be more obvious when we establish that the other two celebrations of the Jewish and Christian autumn cycle correspond to each other.

Character of the Feast of the Epiphany The Jewish feast of Tabernacles was originally an agricultural feast of autumn, which the Jews soon linked to an event in their history, the sojourn in the desert. It has always been a joyful feast celebrated with dancing. The Pharisees attached utmost importance to it, introducing popular elements into it that give it a spectacular and festive tone: Branches of palm were gently shaken, flutes were played, and in the women's courtyard of the Temple, gigantic candelabra were lit that gave so much light that "there was no courtyard in the whole city that was not lit up." The most influential people would dance around the candelabra.

Alongside this element of light was the equally important element of water. It was autumn, and the Jews were waiting for rain. In order to make things propitious, they would go to Cedron and would pour libations of water on the altar. Jesus took part in this feast, at which time, on seeing the people pass by with containers of water, he was moved to say: "Let anyone who is thirsty come to me, and let the one who believes in me drink" (John 7:37).

The early church used to call Epiphany "the day of lights." We find a description of this feast in the oldest travel itinerary in Palestine written by a pilgrim, Egeria or Etheria (fourth century), which furnishes us with valuable details of the liturgical life at that time, especially during feast days (see J. Wilkenson, *Egeria's Travels* [London: SPCK, 1971]). Egeria writes that it was exactly on the occasion of Epiphany that they used to solemnize the feast with a great abundance of light. Her descriptions show her wonder at beholding Constantine's basilicas and the great light-bearing fixtures that were illuminated during the feast and which were used to accompany the long night procession from Bethlehem to Jerusalem, where they arrived before the sun had risen.

In addition to the element of light in celebrating Epiphany, we discover, especially in the East, the element of water as well. On Epiphany, water used to be blessed in a ceremony that was Palestinian in origin. The Eastern Christians would go to the Jordan, pour jars of balsam into the river, and baptize the catechumens. The reason for baptizing on Epiphany was that this feast celebrated the memory of so many different manifestations of Jesus; first among them was his baptism in the Jordan. (The custom of baptizing on Epiphany has always been disapproved of by Rome; instead, the Roman Church connected baptism with Christ's death and resurrection, and thus with Easter.) Therefore, water and light converge in the symbolism of Epiphany as in the Jewish Feast of the Tabernacles. And we could think that, in those great light-bearing fixtures that fascinated Egeria, there was a reminder of the Temple's lampstands, which were approved of by the Pharisees and disapproved of by the Sadducees.

Christmas Day Christmas as the feast of Christ's birth originated in the West. We find it documented in the fourth century in Rome and assigned to December 25. It seems as though it was intended to replace the pagan feast *dies natalis solis invicti* (the birth of the invincible sun), which was celebrated on the shortest day of the year to signify that at the moment when it seems that darkness has the upper hand, the sun succeeds as victor. The church introduced some similar pagan elements, transforming their character, yet in the church's liturgy it is no longer the physical sun but the sun of justice, Jesus. From Rome the feast spread to Africa and other places, and by the fourth century it was known in the East.

Three Masses are celebrated at Christmas. Originally, there was an extraordinarily solemn liturgy at the basilica of St. Peter; today, the first Mass is celebrated at the basilica of St. Mary Major. Following the construction of a chapel devoted to the manger, which Sixtus III included in the construction of this basilica, there arose the custom of celebrating a Mass at night, similar to the one described by Egeria at Bethlehem. In time, this custom would become consolidated into a tradition: the first Mass celebrated at the manger, and another at St. Peter's. Afterward, a third Mass was introduced, celebrated at the church of St. Anastasia, whose feast used to be on December 25. Initially, that liturgy commemorated this saint; later it took on a Christmas character.

New Year's Day should now be considered the octave of Christmas. Throughout the course of time, we have see this feast of New Year's Day solemnized in various ways: as the octave of Christmas, as the circumcision of the Lord, as the birth of Our Lady and as *officium ad prohibendum ab idolis* (the Office of keeping away idols), in reference to the pagan feast of Saturnalia. Here too the Christian liturgy provided a counter-attraction to pagan ceremonies. In the Middle Ages, New Year's Day had a decidedly Marian stamp; later, it was the commemoration of the octave of Christmas that prevailed. New Year's Day as the commemoration of the circumcision originated in Spain in the eleventh century.

The Feast of the Epiphany The feast of Christmas originated in the West in opposition to the pagan feast of December 25, whereas the feast of the Epiphany originated in the East. At a certain moment, it took shape as an osmosis between the Eastern and Western liturgies: The East adopted December 25 as Christmas, and the West adopted the feast of the Epiphany. This is how the liturgical cycle as we know it came to be constituted, made up of Advent, Christmas and Epiphany.

In the Middle Ages, importance was given predominantly to the birth of Jesus in the flesh, overshadowing the aspect of Epiphany, that is, the manifestation of God who comes. To dwell mainly on the birth of Jesus in the flesh means that the grandeur of the event is limited by being confined to the past. Instead, the true meaning of the Epiphany is in the return of Christ, the Christ who not only has come but who is coming and will come. Christian liturgy never turns only to time that has passed but always fixes its sight on the future. The liturgy for the Christmas-Epiphany cycle highlights three points especially:

1. The Incarnation: The Lord has come.

2. The universal effect of renewal that the incarnation has in relation to persons and the created world: The Lord is coming.

3. The anticipation and desire, made more vivid by the Lord's birth, of the parousia which has now become a certainty. The first coming of the savior assures us that he will come back: The Lord will come.

THE EASTER CYCLE

This is the second cycle of the liturgical year, which presents the mystery of Christ in an aspect different from the one emphasized at Christmas. The Easter cycle places the emphasis on the redemption prepared for in the Old Testament, fulfilled in Christ's sacrifice and resurrection, and actualized in each Christian in the anticipation of its fulfillment at the parousia.

There are two feasts in the Easter cycle: Easter and Pentecost, both of which are found in the Jewish liturgical year. The similarity between Christian and Jewish liturgy, found in the Christmas cycle, appears in the Easter cycle as well.

First, let us look at the Jewish character of Easter and Pentecost. In both feasts, various layers of worship are superimposed; in Easter there are three altogether. A first layer, pastoral in nature, is evident in the sacrifice of the lamb, a reflection of a pastoral society in which the firstborn of the flocks were sacrificed. The second layer, agricultural in nature, is characterized by offering a sheaf of barley, the first crop. To these two layers, which are not perfectly Jewish, a third is added, which is straightforwardly Jewish: the recalling of the essential event in the history of Israel, the Exodus from Egypt.

Jewish Pentecost has a historical and natural character too: It is primarily a feast celebrated in thanksgiving for the closing of the harvest. For Jews, as for Christians, it comes fifty days after Passover. The original agricultural aspect has been superimposed in the course of time by another, historical aspect: Pentecost is the feast that commemorates the gift of the Torah, a feast that completes the celebration of the liberation of the Jews from Egypt. The Torah, we could say, is the *connecting tissue* that unites the Jews to one another. Later texts speak of the Exodus as the moment of "betrothal" between God and Israel, and the giving of the gift of the Torah on Mount Sinai as the "wedding" between God and Israel. This historical aspect of Pentecost is not evident in the Bible, as it is for Easter. The superimposition of the historical layer of Pentecost occurs in a later, postbiblical period.

Scholars maintain that this change actually happened in the synagogue through the influence of the church: For Christians, Pentecost is the feast of the manifestation of the Holy Spirit, who spreads Christ's teaching throughout the world. The Jews too would have liked a feast that commemorated the manifestation of the Word of God, the Torah, and it would have transformed Pentecost in that sense.

This twofold character of the Jewish Pentecost is reflected in the two sets of readings prescribed for that occasion. According to one text, Deuteronomy 16:19ff. was supposed to be read; according to another, the first chapter of Ezekiel and the third chapter of Habakkuk, both of which contain the description of a theophany (manifestation of God). The church kept, until the most recent reform of the lectionary, various readings that no longer corresponded to the Christian feast and that were obviously inherited from the synagogue; for example, the readings for Saturday in the ember weeks of Pentecost: Leviticus 23:9 – 11; 15:17 – 21 and Deuteronomy 26:1 – 11. In this case, the church showed itself more conservative than the synagogue.

As for Passover, for the Jews it is essentially the feast of the crossing of the Red Sea and thus of the liberation from sin. This connection between Jewish Passover and Christian Easter is found in Paul: "For our paschal lamb, Christ, has been sacrificed" (1 Corinthians 5:7). This connection is clear in all the liturgy and in the interpretations of the Fathers. In the Exodus from Egypt, they see a connection with the essential Christian religious reality, namely, the Christian's passage from death to life. Even though on different planes, there is one spirit common to the Jewish and Christian feasts.

These points of contact are not only generic: We find them in several liturgical details, such as the fact that the church and the synagogue in this period used to have various readings in common until the most recent reform of the lectionary. These and other elements common to the Christian and Passover liturgies are documentation of a true liturgical continuity between the synagogue and the church, and they attest to the fact that the church has not forgotten that its liturgy of the word originated in a synagogue, in Nazareth (see Luke 4:16ff.). Elements of this kind are not merely a historical curiosity but clearly show the existence of a common spirituality among Christians and Jews.

Conclusion

IN COMING TO WHAT SHOULD BE THE CONCLUSION
of this work, we are well aware that we are far from arriving
at a point of completion. This is especially due to the fragmentary
treatment of our subject, one example of which is the lack of
any emphasis on the sacraments of holy orders or matrimony.
But besides this, the very nature of these reflections prevents us
from thinking in terms of a "conclusion."

The ABCs are always a point of departure. Our hope is
that these elementary pages may encourage an ongoing reading
of liturgical texts, a supremely rich source for entering into
the Christian mystery, because they are aligned, in a relationship
that is without substitute, with that other life-giving source, the
Bible. In other words, we hope this work may serve not only
as an aid in overcoming a type of approach to liturgy that halts
at the exteriority of the rites, but also as an invitation to enter
into mystagogy.

Mystagogy is that method of reading which, by align-
ing biblical texts and liturgical rites alongside one another, leads
us to discover in them the event of salvation at whose center
dwells the God of history. "The task of mystagogy," writes Mazza,
"consists in leading the attention and the *active participation*
of the faithful from the rite to the event, that is, from what is
seen to what is not seen." The author is paraphrasing Ambrose
of Milan:

> You have seen what you were able to see with the eyes of
> your body, with human perception; you have not seen those
> things which are effected but those which are seen. Those
> which are not seen are much greater than those which are

seen, "For the things which are seen are temporal, but the things which are not seen are eternal."[1]

Mystagogy, Mazza continues, is a "theology of the salvific event narrated in scripture (inasmuch as it is narrative) and participated in within the liturgy."[2] Therefore, rather than "concluding," it is our wish that these pages might serve as a departure point for setting forth along the royal path of mystagogy.

---

1. St. Ambrose, Bishop of Milan, *The Sacraments,* book 1, 10; St. Ambrose, *Theological and Dogmatic Works,* trans. Roy J. Defarrari, in *The Fathers of the Church,* vol. 44 (Washington: Catholic University of America Press, 1963), 272.

2. E. Mazza, "Come la liturgia 'legge' la Scrittura," in *Fondamento Biblico del Linguaggio Liturgico,* ed. R. Falsini (O.R. Milano, 1991), 23.